CW00431393

Per

10 Minute Guide to
Microsoft® Access™

Carl Townsend

alpha
books

A Division of Prentice Hall Computer Publishing

11711 North College Avenue, Carmel, Indiana 46032 USA

© 1993 by Alpha Books

All rights reserved. No part of this book shall be reproduced, stored in a retrieval system, or transmitted by any means, electronic, mechanical, photocopying, recording, or otherwise, without written permission from the publisher. No patent liability is assumed with respect to the use of the information contained herein. While every precaution has been taken in the preparation of this book, the publisher and author assume no responsibility for errors or omissions. Neither is any liability assumed for damages resulting from the use of the information contained herein. For more information, address Alpha Books, 11711 North College Avenue, Carmel, Indiana 46032.

International Standard Book Number: 1-56761-230-x
Library of Congress Catalog Card Number: 93-70624

95 94 93   9 8 7 6 5 4 3 2 1

Interpretation of the printing code: the rightmost number of the first series of numbers is the year of the book's printing; the rightmost number of the second series of numbers is the number of the book's printing. For example, a printing code of 93-1 shows that the first printing of the book occurred in 1993.

Publisher: *Marie Butler-Knight*
Associate Publisher: *Lisa A. Bucki*
Managing Editor: *Elizabeth Keaffaber*
Acquisitions Manager: *Stephen R. Poland*
Development Editor: *Seta Frantz*
Manuscript Editor: *Barry Childs-Helton*
Cover Designer: *Dan Armstrong*
Designer: *Amy Peppler-Adams*
Indexer: *Michael von Hughes*
Production Team: *Diana Bigham, Katy Bodenmiller, Scott Cook, Tim Cox, Mark Enochs, Tom Loveman, Roger Morgan, Juli A. Pavey, Joe Ramon, Carrie Roth, Greg Simsic*

Screen reproductions in this book were created by means of the program Collage Plus from Inner Media, Inc., Hollis, NH.

Special thanks to Kelly Oliver for ensuring the technical accuracy of this book.

Printed in the United States of America

Contents

Introduction

Perhaps you walked in this morning and the Microsoft Access program was installed on your computer. Your boss wants you to use this database program to create address files, control inventory, or manage information about employees. What do you do?

A few things are certain:

- You need to find your way around Access readily and efficiently.

- You need to identify and learn the procedures necessary to complete a task or accomplish a goal.

- You need a clear-cut, plain-English guide to the basic features of the program.

You need the *10 Minute Guide to Microsoft Access*.

What Is Microsoft Access?

Microsoft Access is a popular *database management system* (DBMS). You might think that a database program would be hard to use, but you are in for a nice surprise.

Microsoft took the anxiety out of learning and doing database management, and created an easy-to-use system called Microsoft Access. This program is so easy to use that you can be doing productive work in a few minutes—using your computer to organize, store, retrieve, manipulate, and print information.

With Microsoft Access, you can:

• Enter and update your data.

• Quickly find the data you need.

• Organize the data in meaningful ways.

• Create reports, forms, and mailing labels quickly from your data.

• Share data with other programs on your system.

The lessons in this book will show you how to use these Access features.

What Is the 10 Minute Guide?

The *10 Minute Guide* series is a new approach to learning computer programs. Instead of trying to cover the entire program, the *10 Minute Guide* teaches you only about the features of Microsoft Access used most often. Each *10 Minute Guide* is organized in lesson format and contains more than 20 short lessons.

No matter what your professional demands, the *10 Minute Guide to Microsoft Access* will help you find and learn the main features of the program, and get productive with it, more quickly. You can learn this wonderfully logical and powerful program in a fraction of the time you would normally spend to learn a program.

If you haven't yet installed Microsoft Access on your computer, see the inside front cover for instructions.

At the end of this book, there's a table of features, giving you a list of menus and options you can use.

Conventions Used in This Book

Each of the lessons in this Guide includes step-by-step instructions for performing a specific task. The following icons will help you identify particular types of information:

Timesaver Tips These offer shortcuts and hints for using the program effectively.

Plain English These identify new terms and their definitions.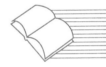

Panic Button These appear in places where new users often run into trouble.

Specific conventions in this book help you to easily find your way around Microsoft Access:

What you type appears in bold, color computer type.

What you select appears in color type.

Menu, Field, and Key names appear with the first letter capitalized.

On-screen text (characters you see on your screen) will appear in computer type.

Selection letters (letters you press to pull down menus and activate options) are printed in bold type.

Trademarks

All terms mentioned in this book that are known to be trademarks have been appropriately capitalized. Alpha Books cannot attest to the accuracy of this information. Use of a term in this book should not be regarded as affecting the validity of any trademark or service mark.

Lesson 1

Getting Started

In this lesson, you'll learn some basic database concepts, as well as how to start Microsoft Access, examine the basic startup screen, and quit.

Database Concepts

If you are new to working with databases, here are some basic concepts:

- *Database*   A collection of objects for managing facts and figures. A database could be used for keeping track of a videotape library, an inventory, a customer list, or a Christmas card list. A database contains one or more tables, as well as other objects (such as reports). An Access database is stored as a single file.

- *Table*   An object in a database that stores facts and figures in two-dimensional form, in rows and columns.

- *Field*   A category of information in a table, such as an address, tape title, or customer ID. Fields correspond to the columns of a table.

- *Record* A collection of all facts and figures relating to an item in a table. Records correspond to the rows.

- *Object* An identifiable unit in a database, such as a table, query, report, or form.

More concepts will be introduced in later chapters.

You can think of a database management system as a filing cabinet. Each database is like a hanging folder in the cabinet; the various objects (including the tables) are like manila folders in the hanging folder.

Starting Microsoft Access

Before using Microsoft Access, you must install it on your computer (see the inside front cover). Once Microsoft Access is installed, you should be able to start it from Windows.

First Things First Before you can install Microsoft Access, you must have Windows already installed and started. You must install Microsoft Access from Windows. If you are not familiar with basic Windows navigation, see the Windows Primer in the back of the book for further instructions.

Start Windows by typing WIN at the DOS prompt (see the Windows Primer for more information). Program Manager will start automatically under Windows. Make the Microsoft Access group active by clicking on its *group icon* (see Figure 1.1), or by highlighting the group with the arrow keys and pressing Enter. If the group is not visible, select it from Program Manager's Window menu. Then start Microsoft Access in either of two ways:

- Double-click on the Microsoft Access icon.

- Highlight the icon with the arrow keys, and press Enter.

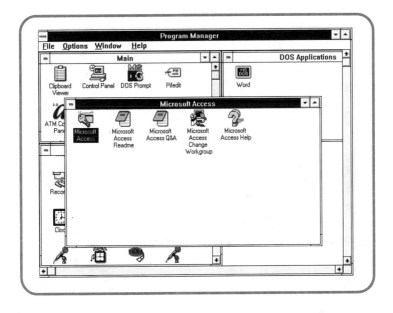

Figure 1.1 The Microsoft Access program group.

Microsoft Access will start, displaying a Microsoft Access *startup window*. Its menu bar will contain two options: **F**ile and **H**elp (see Figure 1.2). Its tool bar contains a single button, a question mark. From this startup window, you can create or open a database, or perform basic database management.

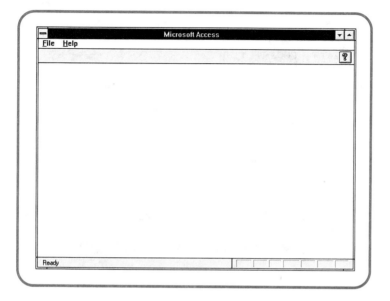

Figure 1.2   The Microsoft Access startup window.

Quitting Microsoft Access

To quit Microsoft Access, double-click on the Control menu box or press Alt+F4.

In this lesson, you learned some basic database concepts, as well as how to start and quit Microsoft Access. The next lesson introduces you to the Main menu and discusses some of its options.

Lesson 2

The Startup
Main Menu

In this lesson, you will get a brief look at the startup Main menu options, learn how the menu bar works, get an introduction to the tool bar, and find out how to get help.

Introduction to the Menu Bar

Microsoft Access uses *dynamic menus*; the options on the menu bar change, depending on how you are using the program. When you first start the program, there are only two options: **File** and **Help**. Once you open a database, you will see the menu bar change, and there will be more options.

Selecting Menu Options
with the Mouse

Using a mouse is the fastest way to navigate Microsoft Access. You can practice using the mouse by following these steps:

1. Move the mouse pointer over the desired menu name on the main menu bar and press the left button. The menu will open. For example, click on File.

2. Click on the desired option in the menu. For example, click on Open Database.

3. If a dialog box like the one in Figure 2.1 opens, select the desired options in the dialog box or enter the desired text (see the Appendix). You can use the Tab or Shift+Tab keys to move between options in the dialog box.

4. Close the dialog box by clicking on OK, and the action will be initiated. For now, click Cancel to close the dialog box without taking any action.

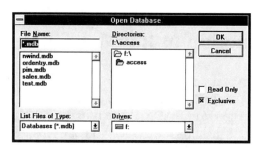

Figure 2.1   A sample dialog box.

Click   To press and release the left mouse button. *Double-click* means to press the left button twice in rapid succession.

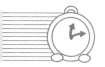

New to Windows?   If you are a new user of Windows and Windows applications, see the Appendix titled "Windows Primer" at the end of this book for more information.

Using the Keyboard with Microsoft Access

The keyboard is used to type text into a dialog box or database table. You may find the keyboard useful for activating menu commands, though it might be less efficient than the mouse. Here is how to use the keyboard to initiate commands:

1. Press the Alt key and then press the highlighted letter of the desired menu name.

2. When the drop-down menu is displayed, press the highlighted letter of the desired option.

I have explained both the keyboard and mouse selection methods in this lesson. During the rest of the book, I will give instructions on only the mouse method.

Using Special Keys

A number of keys function as shortcuts for certain operations in Microsoft Access. For example, there are shortcut keys to cancel an operation, cut or copy text, and close the program.

Table 2.1 The Microsoft Access shortcut keys.

Key	Function
Alt+F4	Close Microsoft Access
Alt+−	Select the Control menu of the document window
Alt	Set the Menu mode (for keyboard menu operations)

continues

7

Table 2.1 Continued.

Key	Function
Enter	Initiate the selected command
Esc	Cancel menu
F1	Initiate the Help system
Shift+F1	Initiate context-sensitive Help
Ctrl+F10	Maximize the document window
Ctrl+X	Cut to the Clipboard
Ctrl+C	Copy to the Clipboard
Ctrl+V	Paste from the Clipboard
Del	Clear
Shift+F2	Zoom in
F5	Move to the record number box
F6	Open a property sheet from a table design
Ctrl+F6	Cycle between open windows
F7	Open the Find dialog box
F9	Recalculate the window fields
Shift+F9	Re-query the underlying table
F11	Return to the database window
Shift+F12	Save a database object
Ctrl+Break	Cancel a query, filter, or find operation
Ctrl+'	Insert the same value as in the previous record
Ctrl+;	Insert the current date
Ctrl++	Add a new record
Ctrl+Enter	Add a new line to memo field

Introduction to the Tool Bar

Just under the menu bar is a *tool bar* with various *buttons* that can simplify tasks. Like the menu options, these change depending on the operations you are performing. We will introduce these buttons throughout the book as you need them. For now, note the single Help button (see Figure 2.2) which appears in the startup window.

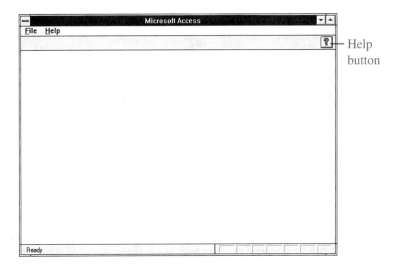

Figure 2.2   The Help button.

Getting Help

You can get help at any time by pressing the F1 key, choosing Help on the menu bar, or clicking on the Help button on the tool bar. Choosing **Contents** from the **Help** menu will open a Help Table of Contents (see Figure 2.3), enabling you to get help on any topic. Double-clicking the upper-left Control menu box of this window (or selecting Exit from the File menu) will close the Help window.

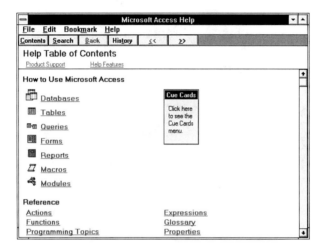

Figure 2.3   The Help window.

If you want help about a specific command, it is often easier to use the *context-sensitive Help*. To use this mode, select the command with the keyboard, but don't activate it with the Enter key as you normally would. Instead, press Shift+F1.

Need Help on a Command?   *Context-sensitive help* is a feature that gives you more information on-screen about how to use the current command.

Another method of getting help is to use the Cue Cards that are part of Microsoft Access. These electronic tutorials guide you through various processes, such as creating a database. To use the Cue Cards:

1. Choose Help from the Main menu.

2. Select Cue Cards from the Help menu.

3. Now you can select options such as help on creating a database (see Figure 2.4).

The Cue Cards lie on top of the normal Microsoft Access windows. While you continue working with the program, the Cue Cards guide you.

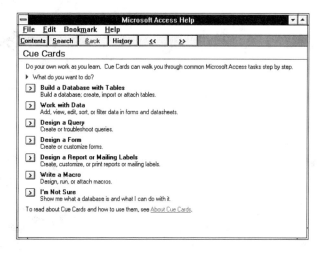

Figure 2.4   Getting help with Cue Cards.

In this lesson, you were introduced to the startup Main menu options; you also learned how the menu bar works and how to get help. Now let's create a database.

Creating a Database

In this lesson, you will learn how to create a database for tables, reports, and other objects.

Plan Your Database

Suppose you've just been given the task of tracking an important mailing list for your organization: a prospect list for the salespeople. Microsoft Access is a good choice for managing this prospect list. It's easy to use, the salespeople can learn it quickly, and it has all the features we need. Let's see how it's done!

Your first step is to define a database. Once that is done, you can decide what tables, reports, forms, and queries are needed. This example is a very simple database; a single table and a few reports will manage the prospects.

Tables in Databases   In the preceding example, the prospects' addresses can be put in a *table*, a Microsoft Access object that stores the information in rows and columns. Then the table can be stored in the database (which is, as you'll recall, a single file). You can add reports and forms to this same *database file*.

Records and Fields in Tables In a Microsoft Access table, the rows are called *records* and the columns are called *fields*.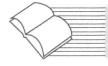

The more complex the environment, the better your database design will be if you follow these general rules:

- Look at how the information is currently managed.

- Define the new objectives, and build from them.

- Avoid putting too much information in a single table.

If you are building a system for tracking orders (for example), you could put customers' addresses in a separate table; that way the order table need not duplicate them in every order. You might put an order's line items in another table, so that every line-item record does not duplicate the entire order. Microsoft Access will then permit you to link the three tables together, so they appear to act as one.

Creating Your Own Database

Now that you've learned how the menu works, let's create a database as a first step in managing your data for reports and labels. Each database file will store tables, queries, reports, and forms associated with the database.

To create a new database, follow these steps:

1. Choose New Database from the File menu. The New Database dialog box is displayed (see Figure 3.1).

2. In the File Name text box, type the name for your new database. The name is limited to eight characters. (The default name is `db1.mdb`. You need not type the extension.)

3. (Optional) If you want to save the database in a different directory, click on (or Tab to) the Directories list box, and select the desired directory. To select a directory, click on it, or scroll to it using the arrow keys.

4. (Optional) If you want to save the database on a different drive, Tab to (or click on) the Drives list box. To display the drives, press Alt+↓, or click on the down arrow. Click on the drive you want, or use the arrow keys to select it.

5. Press Enter or click on OK.

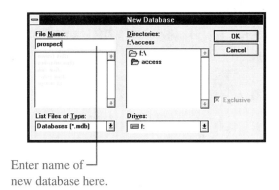

Enter name of
new database here.

Figure 3.1   Entering the name of the new database.

Once the database is created, a Database window appears on-screen (see Figure 3.2). The new database is open; you can use the displayed window to add tables, reports, and other objects to the database, and use any objects already created. Notice the list box in the dialog box is empty. You have not yet created any tables, forms, or reports. Also notice that you now have more menu options on the menu bar, and buttons on the tool bar.

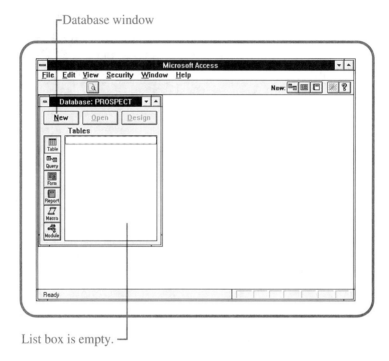

Figure 3.2   The Database window.

What Happened to Those Buttons?   The Design and Open buttons are dim at this time because no objects have been created in the database yet.

Closing the Database

Closing the database ensures all objects are properly stored in the database, and returns you to the startup window. To close the database, choose Close Database on the File menu. The startup window appears again; if you wish, you can open another database or create a new one.

Some Cautions About Closing Closing the database makes sure everything is stored on the disk properly. Only one database can be open at a time in the program. If your database is damaged, see Lesson 21.

In this lesson, you learned how to create and close a database. In the next lesson, you will learn how to create a simple table to hold data.

Lesson 4

Creating a
Simple Table

In this lesson, you'll learn how to create a simple table to hold your data.

Designing a Table

First you need to define what information you want to put in the table. For now, let's look at a database for managing sales prospects. The database will have a single table with the prospects' addresses. All we really need to store now is the name, full address, phone number, a tickle date, a region code, and sales totals for the last six months.

Review: What a Table Is   As you'll recall, a *table* is an object you create in your Access database. You use it to organize information into rows and columns. The rows are called *records* and the columns are called *fields*.

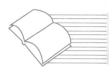

Tickle Date   The *tickle date* is the date when the salesperson should call that person again.

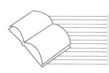

Keep It Simple Keep the database simple. Don't try to put everything you know about the prospect in the file. Decide what data you need to accomplish your purpose, and in what form it should be. Once you have started entering data, you can redefine the database structure as needed for additional data. It's still a good rule, however, to plan ahead as much as possible. It's easier to enter all data for a record at one time than try to add something to each record later.

When you design your table, identify a type of item that will be unique for each record in the table, such as a Social Security number, membership number, or model number for an inventory. Make this unique item the first field in the record; it will be used later as the *primary key*. Access uses the primary key field to *index* your database (see "Setting the Primary Key" later in this lesson). For our example, we'll use the first field to give each person an identification number. The first field will be our primary key field.

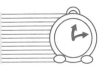 **What's in a Name?** Don't use a person's name for your primary key field. There could be two people in your database with the same name, and Access won't allow two primary key fields to have exactly the same information.

Creating a Table

Now let's create a table for our prospects. If you have already created a database using the steps in the last chapter, use the following steps to open that database:

1. Choose Open Database from the File menu.

2. Choose your database from the File Name list.

3. Click on OK or press Enter. The empty database will appear in the window (see Figure 4.1).

Creating a Database   If you have not yet created a database, create one (and name it PROSPECT) by choosing New Database from the File menu, typing PROSPECT in the File Name text box, and choosing OK.

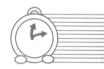

Click here to create a new table.

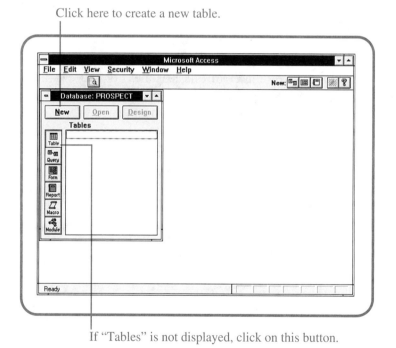

If "Tables" is not displayed, click on this button.

Figure 4.1   The Database window.

Be sure the word Tables is displayed over the list window in the dialog box. If it is not displayed, click on the Table button on the left side of the dialog box (see Figure 4.1). To create a new table, choose the New button by clicking on it or pressing Alt+N. Microsoft Access opens a Table window in Design view (see Figure 4.2). You can use this window to create the structure of your table.

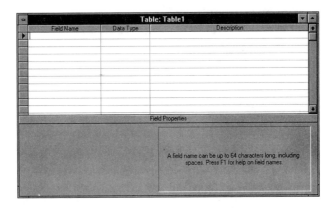

Figure 4.2 Design view for a new window.

You define a table by telling Access what the structure of the table will be. The structure of a table is made up of *fields*. Each field must have a field name, as in PHONE# or LNAME. You must also specify a certain type of data for each field, such as Text or Number. You can also enter a simple description if you want. Access supports eight data types:

- *Text*—text and numbers that aren't used in calculations.

- *Memo*—long text strings (multiple sentences).

- *Date/Time*—dates and times.

- *Number*—numbers used in calculations.

- *Currency*—currency values.

- *Counter*—an integer which is incremented automatically.

- *Yes/no*—logical values that can be true or false.

For our mailing list, use the following fields:

Field Name	Type	Description
ID	Number	Identification Number
LNAME	Text	Last Name
FNAME	Text	First Name
ADDRESS	Text	Address
CITY	Text	City
ST	Text	State
ZIP	Number	ZIP Code
TICKLE	Date	Call-back date
PHONE	Number	Telephone number
REGION	Number	Region
SALES	Number	Sales for last six months

To create the database structure, follow these instructions:

1. If necessary, move the cursor to the first field's text box, and enter a field name (for the example, ID).

2. Press Enter or Tab to move to the Data Type column.

21

3. A default value of Text will be entered. If you want to use Text as the data type, simply press Enter, or Tab to the next column. If you want a different data type, click on the down arrow, or press Alt+↓ to open the Data Type list box. (For this example, choose Number from the list box.)

4. If necessary, press Enter (or Tab to the last column) and type in a description for the field. For the example, type in Identification number.

5. Press Enter (or Tab to the next row), and type in the information for the second field. Continue until all the fields you need have been defined.

Setting Field Properties

Each field has certain *properties* you must set. You have already named each field; for now, the only properties you need to set are the format properties of the ID, ZIP, TICKLE, REGION, and SALES fields. The text fields do not need to be set. To set the properties, follow these steps:

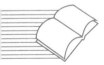

Property A property of a field is a particular characteristic such as size, color, or name.

1. To set the ID field's size, click on any box in the row that defines the ID field. The Field Properties box at the bottom of the screen will display the current field's properties (see Figure 4.3).

2. Click on the Field Size box; you'll see an arrow pop up. Click on it (or press Alt+↓) to display your options.

3. Choose Long Integer to use whole numbers only.

22

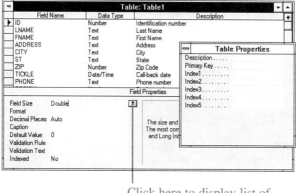

Click here to display list of
property options.

Figure 4.3   The Properties list.

4. Click on any box in the ZIP row, and change the field
   size to Long Integer by repeating steps 2 and 3.

5. Click on any box in the REGION row, and change the
   field size to Integer.

6. To set the TICKLE field's format, click on any box in
   the TICKLE row, and click on the Format property box.

7. To open the list box, click on the arrow (or press Alt+↓);
   choose Medium Date.

8. To set the SALES format, click on any box in the
   SALES row, and click on the Format property box.

9. Open the list box, and select Currency.

Setting the Primary Key

For the next step, you should set the primary key. The value in this field will be unique for each record, which permits faster access to the table. Microsoft Access does this by creating an index on the primary key field. To set the primary key, follow these steps:

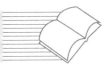

Indexing   Organizing or sorting a database's records according to the content of one or more fields is called *indexing* the database.

1. Select Table Properties from the View menu to view the current indexes (there are none).

2. Click anywhere in the first row (in our example, this is the ID row).

3. Click on the Primary key button in the tool bar, or select Set Primary Key from the Edit menu. A key icon will appear in the row selector area to the left of the first field (see Figure 4.4).

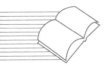

Row Selector   The small triangle to the left of the first field of the database is called the *row selector*. Clicking on any field in a row will move the triangle to that row.

Selecting Multiple Fields   You can select multiple fields for the primary key. Hold down the Ctrl key while clicking on the row selector for each field you want to include. After each row is highlighted, click on the Primary Key button. A key icon will appear in each highlighted row.

Key icon   Primary key button

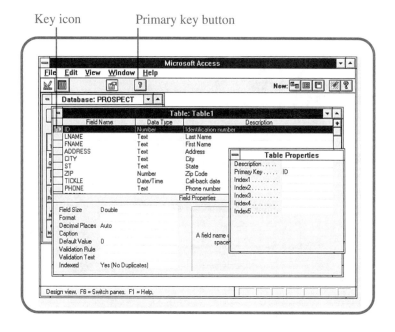

Figure 4.4   Setting the primary key.

If you have not selected a primary key when you save the table, Access will ask you if you want to create one before it saves the table. If you answer Yes, a new Counter type field will be created, and it will be used as the primary key field. If you already have a field for counter type, it will be chosen as the primary key field.

Now each time you redisplay the table (as you would do when switching from Design to Database view), it will be reordered by primary key fields (in our example, by ID number).

Saving the Table

Once the table is finished, save it by following these steps.

1. Choose the Save As command from File menu.

2. Enter the name for the table (see Figure 4.5).

3. Choose OK or press Enter.

Figure 4.5   Saving a table.

Closing a Table

To close a table, choose Close from the File menu. If any changes have been made since you last saved the table, Microsoft Access will prompt you to save the table. You are returned to the Database window, with the new table displayed in the list.

In this lesson, you learned how to create a table, set field properties, save the table, and close it. In the next lesson, you will learn how to add data to the table.

Lesson 5

Adding Data to a Table

In this lesson, you will learn how to add records to a table, edit them, and print them.

Opening the Table

In the last two lessons, you've created your database and added a table. Now it's time to place your facts and figures into their appropriate fields of the table. Every time you enter a complete row of fields, you have entered one complete record into the database.

Before you can add records to a table, you must open the database (if it is not already open) and the table. To open a database, choose Open Database from the File menu. Select the desired database and choose OK.

Quick Return to the Window If a database is open, a Database window will be displayed. A title bar will show the name of the database, though the window may be hidden under another window. Press the F11 key to return quickly to any open Database window.

Once you have opened a database (such as the one you created in earlier lessons), examine the Database window. Be sure the word Tables is displayed at the top of the list box. If not, click on the Tables button to the left of the list box. The list now displays the current tables in the database. Select the desired table (such as PROSPT), and then select Open or double-click on the table name. The table will open, showing empty rows and columns like a spreadsheet (see Figure 5.1). This is called the Datasheet view.

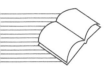

Datasheet View   A *datasheet* is a view of a table that displays the data with the records in rows and the fields in columns.

When viewing tables, you can use either Table **D**esign view or Datasheet view. You can use the two far-left icons on the **V**iew menu to switch between these choices.

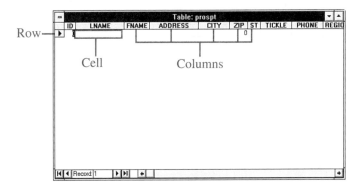

Figure 5.1   An empty datasheet for adding records.

Adding Records

If you have just created a table, there will be no records in the table. To add a record to the datasheet, fill in the cells for the first row. Use the Tab key, the Enter key, or the arrow keys to move the cursor between the columns as you fill in the data. Pressing Shift+Tab will move you backward through the columns. After completing the entry of a record, use the Tab key to move to the first field of the next row, and enter that record. Continue until you have added all the records you want to add (see Figure 5.2).

Current record

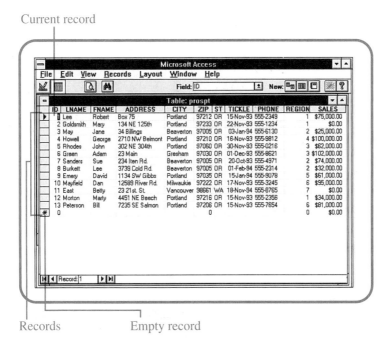

Records   Empty record

Figure 5.2   The datasheet after entering a few records.

Adding Records to Existing Records in a Table

If a table already contains records, any records you add will be placed at the end of the datasheet. For example, open the PROSPT table (if it isn't already open). At the end of the datasheet, you will see an asterisk marking a blank or empty record. To add a record, you would fill out this record, which in turn opens another record.

In the record selection area to the left of the first field, a right triangle marks the current record. If a blank record is entered accidentally here, delete it by selecting it and then choosing Undo Current Record from the Edit menu. Close the table and database when you are through adding records.

Saving Records

Microsoft Access saves your records to disk as you enter them. Each time you move the cursor to the next record, the program saves the record you just entered (or changed), automatically.

Printing a Datasheet

Sometimes it's easier to look at your datasheet on paper, rather than scrolling through it screen by screen on your monitor. You can print your datasheet by following these steps:

1. Make sure your datasheet is in the active window.

2. Select Print from the File menu.

3. A dialog box will appear, showing the options listed in Table 5.1.

4. When you're finished selecting options, choose OK. The table will be printed.

Table 5.1   The Print dialog box options.

Option	Description
All	Prints the entire datasheet.
Selection	Prints only the selection you have highlighted.
Pages	Prints only certain pages.
From	Use this box to enter the first page to print.
To	Use this box to enter the last page to print.
Print **Q**uality	A number, followed by dpi (dots per inch). A higher number means a better print quality.
Print to File	A check in this box means the datasheet will be printed to a file, not to paper.
Copies	Type the number of copies you want.
Collate Copies	Collates pages if you select more than one copy.

Print Preview   If you want to see what your datasheet will look like before it's printed, select Print Preview from the File menu, or click on the Print Preview button on the tool bar. You can view different pages by clicking on the arrows at the bottom left of the window. To exit, press Esc.

You can use the Print Setup dialog box to change other options. This dialog box will be displayed if you select Setup from the Print dialog box or Print Setup from the File menu.

Using this dialog box, you can change any of the options shown in Table 5.2.

Table 5.2   The Print Setup dialog box options.

Option	Description
Default Printer	When selected, Access prints to the default printer.
Specific Printer	When selected, Access prints to the printer of your choice.
Portrait	Prints the datasheet across the narrow width of the paper.
Landscape	Prints the datasheet across the wide width of the paper.
Size	Select the size of paper to use.
Source	Specify whether you want to print from the paper tray or from your own paper (manual feed).
Margins	Specify Left, Right, Top, or Bottom margins.
Data Only	A check in this box will tell Access to print only the data on the datasheet (no embedded objects).

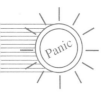

Can't Print?   Access will display the **P**rint command in the File menu only if you are in Datasheet view. To change to Datasheet view, select Datasheet from the View menu, or click on the Datasheet View button on the tool bar.

Closing a Table

When you have finished entering data, you should close the table and database. This will ensure that everything is saved to the disk properly and no data is lost. To close the table, follow these steps:

1. Choose Close from the File menu. The table will be saved to the disk and will no longer be displayed.

2. When you are through with the database itself, close it by choosing Close Database from the File menu.

A Word to the Wise   Although Microsoft Access saves the records as you enter them, a wise computer user will not trust this feature to ensure complete safety. You have no assurance that all your data is on the disk until the database is closed. If you plan to take a break from the computer, close the database; open it again when you return.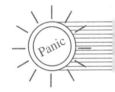

In this lesson you learned how to add records to a table, save the records, and print them. In the next lesson, you will learn how to edit your records.

Lesson 6

Editing Records

In this lesson you will learn how to move around in a datasheet, edit existing records, and move and copy data.

Moving Around in the Datasheet

Once your records are entered, you might discover a few errors that need to be fixed. Fortunately, moving around the datasheet is easy. You can use the shortcut keys in Table 6.1 to move the cursor position.

Table 6.1   Moving around with the keyboard.

Press	To
Tab	Move the cursor from left to right across a record.
Shift+Tab	Move the cursor from right to left.
Arrow keys	Move up, down, right, or left.
PageUp	Scroll up through the datasheet one screen at a time.
PageDown	Scroll down through the datasheet one screen at a time.

Press	To
Home	Move the cursor to the beginning of a record.
End	Move the cursor to the end of a record.
Ctrl+Home	Put the cursor in the far-left field of the first record.
Ctrl+End	Put the cursor in the far-right field on the last record.

You can also use the mouse to click on any field you want to edit. You can click on the arrows in the scroll bars to scroll up, down, left, or right, one row or column at a time. You can also click inside the bar to move one screenful at a time, or drag the scroll box to a new location (see Figure 6.1). When you move the scroll box, the screen moves proportionately.

Figure 6.1 Use the scroll boxes to move around the datasheet.

Editing Existing Records

To edit a record in a datasheet, first select the field in the record you want to edit. Using the mouse, you can position the cursor anywhere in the field. Or you could use the keyboard to move to the field, and do one of two things:

- If the data in the field is highlighted, you can start typing. The highlighted data will be deleted and the new data will replace it.

- If the data in the field is highlighted, but you don't want to delete everything, press F2; this lets you move around in the field with the arrow keys. When you're finished, press F2 again.

Deleting Entire Records

If you want to delete an entire record, click on the row selection box to the far left of the record. An arrow will appear in the box, and the whole record will be highlighted. Select Delete from the Edit menu or press the Delete key. A dialog box will appear asking you to confirm your action. Select OK.

Inserting a Record

Since Access sorts the datasheet by the primary key field, your records are inserted in the proper sequence automatically. If you are using sequential numbers as your primary key fields, you will have to renumber your records to allow for the new record. If you have ten records, for example, and you need to insert a new record as number eight, you would change the primary key fields in records eight, nine, and ten. Then you could simply type in the new record in the bottom row, using the number 8 in the primary key field. When Access saves the datasheet, the records will be in numerical order.

Copying and Moving Data in the Datasheet

You can use the **E**dit menu to simplify your editing by cutting or copying selected material and pasting it. *Cutting* a selection will move the data from the datasheet to the Clipboard. *Copying* a selection will keep the data in its original place, and keep a copy in the Clipboard. To copy the data from the Clipboard, paste it to your datasheet.

The Clipboard   The data you cut or copy is temporarily stored in an area called the *Clipboard* until you paste it into your datasheet. The Clipboard keeps the same information ready for you to paste until you cut or copy something new. This allows you to use the **P**aste command repeatedly without having to cut or copy the same data.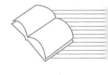

Cutting Versus Deleting   Cutting a selection is different from deleting it. When you *cut* data, it is deleted from the original location, but a copy of it is saved in the Clipboard for later retrieval. If you *delete* data, it is gone for good.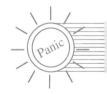

Moving Records

For example, pretend you have a database exactly like the one in Figure 5.2. After typing the records, you realize that Marty Morton's ID number is actually 13, and Bill Peterson is number 12. You would move Marty Morton's record by using the Cut command. Here's how:

1. Highlight the data you want to move. In this case, click on the row selection box to the left of the row to highlight Marty Morton's entire record.

2. Open the Edit menu and select Cut (see Figure 6.2).

3. A dialog box will appear, asking you to confirm your changes. Select OK.

4. To paste the selection to a new location, first you position the cursor in the correct row. In this case, move the cursor to the row beneath Bill Peterson's record.

5. Highlight an area that is exactly the same size as your selection. For this example, you would click on the row selection box to select the entire row.

6. Select Paste from the Edit menu.

To make your sample datasheet correct, all you would have to do now is change the ID numbers for Marty Morton and Bill Peterson.

Select Cut from the Edit menu.

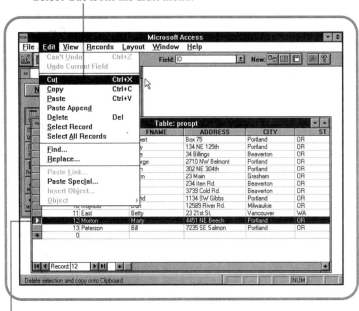

Click on the Row Selector to highlight the entire row.

Figure 6.2   Cutting a selection to the Clipboard.

Copying Records

Copying selected data is similar to cutting it. The only difference is that the data is not deleted from the original location. For example, seven of the people listed on the datasheet in Figure 5.2 live in Portland; instead of typing the city's name time after time, you can paste copies in each City field. You would:

1. Highlight the data you want to copy. In this case, you would highlight Portland after the first time you type it.

2. Select Copy from the Edit menu. Access copies Portland to the Clipboard (see Figure 6.3).

3. Position the cursor in the correct location. For our
   example, your cursor would be in the City field.

4. Be sure that the area you have selected to paste the data
   to is the same size as the area of the data you copied to
   the Clipboard.

5. Select Paste from the Edit menu.

For our example, you could just select Paste every time
you have to enter "Portland," as long as you don't cut or
copy anything else to the Clipboard.

Select Copy from the Edit menu.   The selection to be copied.

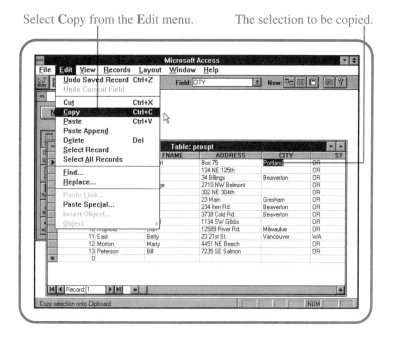

Figure 6.3   Copying a selection to the Clipboard.

Duplicate Records?   If you are copying an entire record to a new location, be sure to change the data in the primary key field. You must have different information in each primary key field so Access can distinguish between records.

Appending Your Selection   If you want to paste your cut or copied data to the end of your datasheet, select Paste Append from the Edit menu. This command will paste your selection to the last empty record in your datasheet, automatically.

In this lesson, you learned how to move around in the datasheet and edit existing records. In the next lesson, you will learn how to edit and rearrange fields in the table structure.

Changing the Structure or the View of a Table

In this lesson, you'll learn how to modify a table's structure by deleting, inserting, and rearranging fields.

Changing the Structure of a Table

Changing the structure of a table does not cause any data loss unless you delete a field, or change the field properties to a format that doesn't support the existing data.

If you want to change a table's structure, first click on the Design View button on the tool bar to put the table in Design view.

Deleting a Field

You may decide you don't need a particular field anymore, and want to delete it from the table. This will save disk space and simplify future data entry.

Fields Versus Records   Don't confuse the terms *field* and *record*. Fields are pieces of information about each item in your database; they are stored as columns in the table. Records identify all the information about a particular item, and are stored as rows. All the information for Dan Mayfield, for example, might be stored as a single record (row). His address, city, state, Zip, and telephone number are all fields in that record.

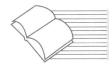

To delete a field, follow these steps:

1. If necessary, open the database by choosing Open Database on the File menu.

2. If necessary, switch the display to Design view by clicking on the Design View button on the tool bar, or by choosing Table Design from the View menu (see Figure 7.1).

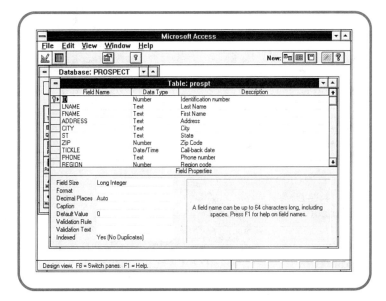

Figure 7.1   Table Design View.

3. Click on the row selector for the row that defines the field to delete (or use the arrow keys, and press Shift+Spacebar to highlight the row selector).

4. Choose Delete Row from the Edit menu or press the Del key.

5. Choose OK.

The field and all data in it will be deleted.

Row Selector   The *row selector* is the triangle pointer in the space just to the left of the first column in the table.

Be Sure   Be sure you have selected the correct field. Once you have deleted the field, all data in that field will be lost, and will not be recoverable. Data in other fields will not be affected.

Inserting a Field

After you have created a table, you may want to add a new field. For example, after creating a database of a club membership, you may decide to add a field later that defines when the member first joined the club. Microsoft Access permits you to add new fields at any time, without losing data in existing fields.

To add a new field:

1. If necessary, switch the display to Design view by clicking on the Design View button on the tool bar, or by choosing Table Design from the View menu (see Figure 7.1).

2. Click on the row selector for the row just below where you want to add the new field (or use the arrow keys and move to the row, then press Shift+Spacebar).

3. Choose Insert Row from the Edit menu or press the Insert key.

4. Define the new field by entering the field name, data type, and description (see Lesson 4).

Rearranging the Fields

There may be times when you want to rearrange the fields in a table. You may want to move a primary field (used for an index) so that you may also use it as the first field, or (in our example database) move the phone number field so it comes before the Tickle field.

1. If necessary, switch the display to Design view by clicking on the Design View button on the tool bar, or by choosing Table Design from the View menu.

2. Select the entire row for the field you want to move.

3. Click and hold the left mouse button on the row selector, and drag the row. When the row is where you want it to be, release the mouse button.

Drag   To move the mouse pointer by holding down the left mouse button and moving the mouse.

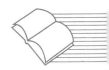

Changing the View of a Table

Changing the *view* of the table affects what you see in the Datasheet view, but doesn't change the basic underlying structure. For example, you can make a column smaller, but the structure doesn't change, and any data in the smaller column is not truncated.

Reordering a Field

Sometimes you may want to change where a field appears on the datasheet, without changing its order in the structure. (For example, you might want to keep a primary key as the first field in the structure, but give it a more convenient location on the datasheet.) To reorder a field's position on the datasheet, follow these steps:

1. With the table in Datasheet view, position the pointer on the field selector (area with the field name above the row). The pointer changes to a downward arrow.

2. Click on the field selector to select the entire field.

3. Click and hold the left mouse button on the field selector, and drag the column to the new position.

4. To deselect the field, click anywhere else in the datasheet.

Resizing a Field or Column

Resizing a field's column width permits you to tighten up the view, which in turn lets you display more data at a time. To resize the column width for a field, follow these steps:

1. Position the pointer to the right of the column you want to resize, on the line between the field titles. The pointer changes to indicate the border can be moved.

2. Drag the line until the column is the desired size.

Resizing a Row You can resize a row in the same way by dragging the line that separates the rows. Note, however, that resizing one row affects all the rows; they all resize at once.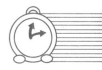

Save Your Changes

You can use Save Layout on the File menu to save the new layout. Once you have modified the database's structure, choose Close Database from the File menu to save your changes.

In this lesson, you learned how to open a table, and how to delete, insert, rearrange, resize, and reorder fields in the table's structure. In the next lesson, you will learn how to create a form.

Lesson 8

Displaying Tables with Forms

In this lesson, you will learn how to create forms and arrange records in forms.

Introduction to Form Creation

Forms permit you to enter, edit, and display data, one record at a time. If you use a Datasheet view to enter records, usually not all the fields will be visible at once. You will have to scroll constantly as you add, edit, and view records. Using forms, on the other hand, lets you see all the fields of a single record at once. This simplifies data entry.

Form   An object you can use to enter, edit, view, or print data records.

Microsoft Access includes a FormWizard button to help you put together forms. This lesson shows you how to use it.

Creating a Form

To create a form, start with the Database window open; click on the Form button (see Figure 8.1) to select the Forms option (the button will turn red). The Database window will then list all the forms in the database (if it's new, none will be listed). Click on the New button in the Database window, and you will get a New Form window (see Figure 8.2).

Click here to
create a new form.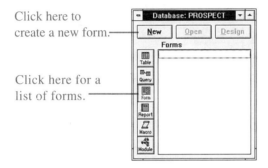

Click here for a
list of forms.

Figure 8.1 The Database window.

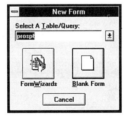

Figure 8.2 The New Form window.

1. In the Select A Table/Query: text box, click on the down arrow at the right (or press Alt+↓). A list box will open, displaying the tables for which you can build forms. (In this example, the only available table is PROSPT.)

49

2. Click on the name of the table for which you want to build a form.

3. Choose the FormWizards button (or press Alt+W).

4. On the first FormWizard screen, you are asked to select an AccessWizard. Choose Single-column and then click on OK or press Alt+O (see Figure 8.3).

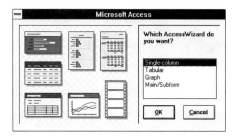

Figure 8.3   Choosing the type of form.

5. On the next screen, you will be asked to select the fields to display in the form (see Figure 8.4). Select >> to move all your fields to the Field order on form: box on the right. Click on Next.

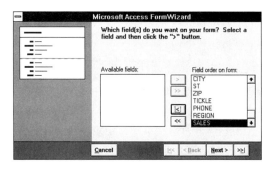

Figure 8.4   Choosing the fields for the form.

6. Select a look for the form by choosing Standard, and then click on Next (see Figure 8.5).

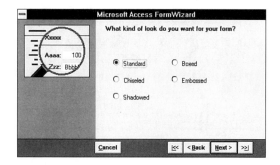

Figure 8.5   Choosing the type of format.

7. On the next screen, enter a title for the form (see Figure 8.6), and click on Open. FormWizard creates the form, and displays the database's first record in it (see Figure 8.7).

Figure 8.6   Entering the form's title.

Label   Text box

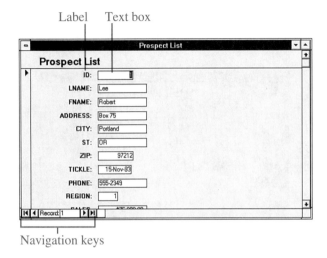

Navigation keys

Figure 8.7   The final form.

Viewing Records with a Form

The form you have created can be used to display (view), add, change, delete, or print records. The various objects on the form are known as controls.

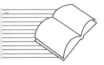

Control   On a form or report, a *control* is an object that displays data from a field, the result of a calculation, a label, graph, picture, or another object.

Areas of the form that are used for input (for text or numbers) are called *text boxes*. Labels identify each text box, as well as a title for the form. There may also be a *check box* on some forms for entering logical values. (The next lesson shows you other types of controls.)

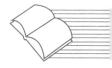

Text box   An area of a form used to enter data.

To view a particular record, use the Go To command on the Records menu, or the navigation buttons at the bottom of the window. To return to a Datasheet view and see multiple records, click on the Datasheet View button on the tool bar, or the Datasheet command on the View menu. You can use the Form View button (or select Form on the View menu) to return to Form view.

Adding Records with a Form

Forms simplify adding records, because the new record's fields are all displayed at the same time. To add a new record with a form displayed, follow these steps:

1. From the Records menu, select Go To. Then select New from the list that appears.

2. Enter the data for each field; Tab to move the cursor between fields. You can press Shift+Tab to move backward through the fields, or you can use the mouse to click on any field.

3. From the last field, press Tab to display an empty form for the next record.

Oops!   Use the Undo Current Field command of the Edit menu if you need to restore a field. To restore a previously typed value, use the Undo Typing command from the Edit menu.

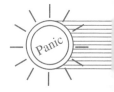

Automatic Saving As you enter or edit records, the previous record you entered or edited is saved automatically. You don't need to do anything else to save records as you enter them.

Saving the Form

Once the form design is completed, you should save the form if you intend to use it in the future. To save an open form, follow these steps:

1. Choose Save Form As from the File menu.

2. Enter the name of the form you want to save. (Avoid using the name of any existing table, query, report, or other form.)

3. Choose OK or press Enter.

Printing Data with a Form

To print data using an open form, follow these steps:

1. Choose Print from the File menu.

2. Click on OK or press Enter. The data will be printed using the form.

Print Preview If you want to see what your form will look like before you print it, select Print Preview from the File menu or click on the Print Preview button in the tool bar. To exit the Print Preview window, press Esc.

Closing a Form

Once you are through using a form, close it to remove it from the screen. To close a form, choose Close from the File menu. The new form's name will be on the list in the Database window.

In this lesson, you learned how to create a form using FormWizard, and how to view a record in the form. In the next lesson, you will learn how to customize a form for your specific needs.

Lesson 9

Creative Form Design

In this lesson, you will learn how to customize forms to meet your specific needs. You will learn how to add, resize, and move the labels and text boxes on the form, customize the text, and add fields to controls.

Modifying a Form Design

Once you have created a form with FormWizard, you may want to change the design. Microsoft Access makes this easy: you simply use the mouse to drag and resize.

To start redesigning a form, open your database and click on the Form button in the Database window. The list of the current forms will be displayed. Highlight the form you want to modify, and choose the Design button (see Figure 9.1). The form will open in Design view (see Figure 9.2).

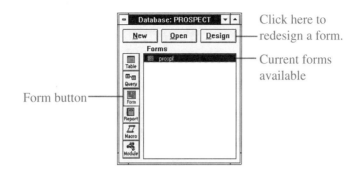

Figure 9.1   The Form window.

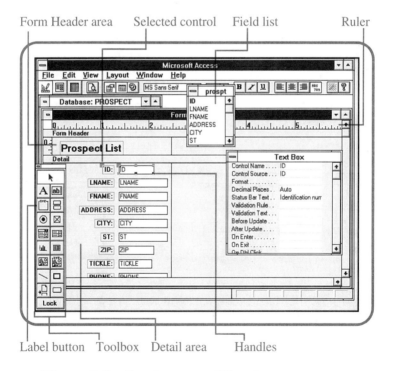

Figure 9.2   Starting to modify a form.

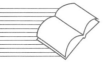

Toolbox Versus Tool Bar   Notice that in Design view a new window called a *toolbox* is displayed. It is a special set of buttons that don't appear on the regular tool bar. You can use these buttons to design forms. You can move the toolbox by dragging its top title bar, and turn it on or off from the View menu.

Notice the differences between this view and a normal form display. The title is now in a separate Form Header area, and an empty Form Footer area has been added. The labels and text boxes are in a Detail area. The tool bar is displayed by default, but you can change your options on the View menu so the Field List or the Properties List is displayed.

Resizing Controls

As you'll recall, each object on the displayed form is called a control. In the Design view, you can move and resize these controls, and add new ones.

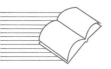

Control   An object on a form or report.

To manipulate a control, you must first select it. To select a text box with a label, for example, click on the associated text box. The text box and its label will be displayed with handles surrounding them (see Figure 9.2).

- To resize the box vertically, drag the top and/or bottom handles.

- To resize a box horizontally, drag the right and/or left handles.

- To resize a box horizontally and vertically at the same time, drag the diagonal handles.

You can use the rulers to align your work. The rulers should be displayed by default, but if they aren't, you can select them from the **V**iew menu.

More Than One   You can select more than one control at a time by holding down the Shift key while selecting.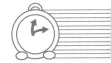

Moving Controls

Microsoft Access permits you to move a text box and its associated label, together or separately. To move them separately, select the control, then drag the large handle in the upper left corner (this is known as the *move handle*). When you move the text box or label separately, the mouse pointer will look like a pointing hand.

To move the text box and label together, click on the control until the pointer looks like a hand with the palm showing. Now drag the text box and its label to the new position.

Use Multiple Selections to Align   To maintain the current alignment while you are moving multiple controls, select them together, and then move them.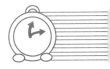

Adding a Label

A *label* is simply text added to the form to display information. The *title* already on the form is one type of label. You can add additional labels (such as your company name) to the form.

To add a label, use the special toolbox that appears the first time you open a form in Design view. If it is not already displayed, you can get it by choosing Toolbox from the View menu. Click on the Label button in the first row of the toolbox. Move the mouse pointer to the form, click on the appropriate place, and enter the text for the label.

Customizing Text

You can modify any text by changing the font, size, color, alignment, and attributes (normal, bold, and italic). To change the appearance of text in a control, follow these steps:

1. Select the control you want to modify. If it contains text, the tool bar will display additional buttons for modifying the text (see Figure 9.3).

2. To change the attributes, click on the Bold, Underline, or Italic buttons in the tool bar.

3. To change the alignment, click on the Left, Center, or Right buttons in the tool bar.

4. If you want to change the font and font size, set them from the tool bar.

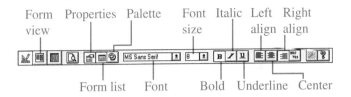

Form view | Properties | Palette | Font size | Italic | Left align | Right align

Form list | Font | Bold | Underline | Center

Figure 9.3   Modifying text using the tool bar.

After you have completed your work, resize the label to the new text by choosing Size to Fit from the Layout menu. Now you can modify the color of the text as needed.

To set the color of the text, follow these steps:

1. Click on the Palette button, or select Palette from the View menu.

2. From the Palette window (see Figure 9.4), you can set the color of the text, or you can set separate colors for fill and outline (simply click on the color of your choice). You can also set the appearance of the text and the border width (normal, raised, or sunken).

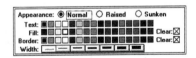

Figure 9.4   The Palette window.

Using a List Box with a Form

Sometimes it's faster and easier to select a preset choice from a list box than to type in text. For example, in our sample database, all customers live in one of five different cities. For the sake of this example, let's assume that all of your future prospects will also live in one of those cities. If you want to be able to choose the name of the city quickly, and be sure it's spelled right, it's a good idea to select it from a list box.

To create a list box for your city field, follow these steps:

1. Clear an area with sufficient room for the list box. In our example, you would delete the city field (select the text box and the label and press the Delete key), select the fields beneath it (press the Shift key as you click on them), and move them down an inch or so.

2. Click on the List Box button in the tool bar.

3. Your mouse pointer will look like a plus sign (+) when you move it to the Detail area. When you hold down the left mouse button and drag the mouse, you are creating the shape of your list box (see Figure 9.5).

4. If the controls are the wrong size (or in the wrong place), fix them using what you learned earlier in this lesson.

5. If the Properties box is not displayed, click on the Properties button or select Properties from the View menu.

6. Click on the list box so that its properties are displayed.

Properties button   This is the shape of the list box.

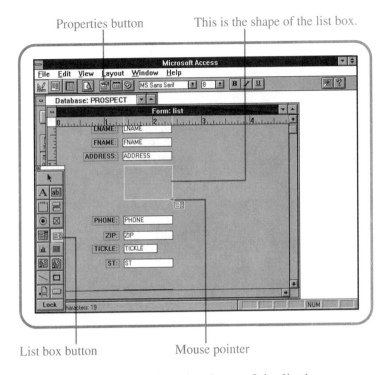

List box button   Mouse pointer

Figure 9.5 Creating the shape of the list box.

7. Change the appropriate properties (see Figure 9.6). For our example, change:

- the Control Name to `CITY`.

- the Row Source Type to `Value List`.

- the Row Source to
  `Portland;Beaverton;Gresham;Vancouver;Milwaukie.`

What Goes in the List Box?   You can't simply type your choices into the list box. You have to enter them in the Properties box under Row Source. When entering your choices, use semicolons (without spaces) to separate them.

Properties button   The list box is selected.   Properties list box

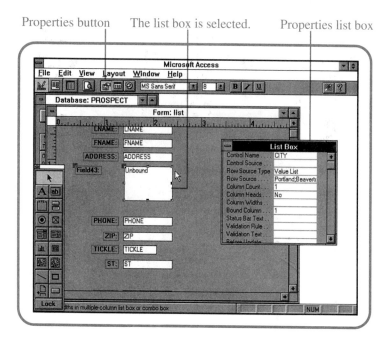

Figure 9.6   Changing the properties of a list box.

8. Your label might be wrong, but you can edit it. For our example, change the label to `CITY`.

To see how your new list box looks in the form, click on the Form View button or select Form from the View menu (see Figure 9.7). If the form doesn't look right, you can go back to Design view and change it. If you have scroll bars in your list box and you don't want them, you can make your list box longer by resizing it in Design view.

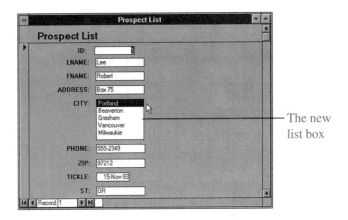

Figure 9.7 The completed list box.

List Versus Combo Instead of making a list box, you might want to make a *combo box*, so you are not restricted to preset choices. A combo box lets you type a value or choose from the list. To make one, select the Combo Box icon from the tool bar, and follow the steps for making a list box. When you use a combo box, your choices aren't displayed automatically; you have to select the down arrow button to see them.

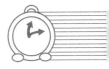

Save It! Be sure to save the form if you want to keep it; use Save from the File menu. Close the form when you are through using it, using Close on the File menu.

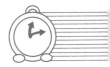

In this lesson, you have learned how to customize a form to meet your specific needs. In the next lesson, you will learn how to query your database for information.

65

Lesson 10

Querying a Database

In this lesson, you'll learn how to query a database.

Introduction to Queries

Most of the time you will want specific information when using a database. You won't want to look at the entire database when making a decision. The PROSPECT database for sales (for example) might contain hundreds of names, each with its own tickle date entered from the previous call. Suppose, as a salesperson, you want only the names that have today's tickle date. To get them, you must build a query to access the database and retrieve only the names that meet this criterion. Then you can print a report from the query, containing only names and phone numbers.

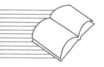

What's a Query? A *query* works much like a question directed at a database. In effect, it asks (for example), "Which prospects have today's tickle date?" The query also has a *condition* included, such as "What records have a tickle date *equal to* today's date?"

Creating a Query

Now's let's create a simple query for getting today's prospects from the PROSPECT database, using the tickle date.

1. If the database is not open already, open it so that the Database window is displayed.

2. Choose the Query icon. The list window (see Figure 10.1) will display any current queries on the database. (In this example, there are none.)

3. To create a new query, choose the New button on the Database window. An Add Table dialog box is displayed (see Figure 10.2).

4. Select the table(s) you want to use for the query (in this example, the PROSPT table). If you want more than one, choose Add after each one. After the last table is selected, choose Close.

5. The fields of the table are displayed in a list box in the Query window. Any field that is used for a primary key is in boldface. Using the mouse, drag the fields you want to see in the query to the Field row of the Query window (see Figure 10.3). In this example you would drag TICKLE, LNAME, FNAME, PHONE, and RE-GION one at a time to the Field row. Place the fields in the columns, in the same order you want them to follow in the query.

Add Fields Fast   You can also use the drop-down list in each Field cell to add a field.

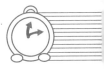

6. Click on the Datasheet View button to see the results of the query. (You can see the button in Figure 10.3.)

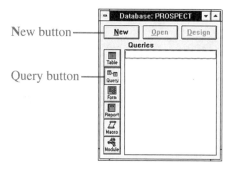

Figure 10.1   The Database window.

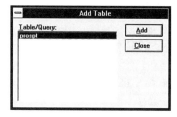

Figure 10.2   Adding tables for the query.

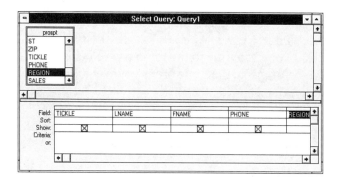

Figure 10.3   The fields of the table that are available for selection.

Figure 10.4 shows the results of the query. These results are known as a *dynaset*.

Datasheet View button

Figure 10.4   The results of the query.

Dynaset   When you select Datasheet view after you design the query, you are looking at a *dynaset*— a dynamic set of the records that you asked for in the query. It is considered *dynamic* because the query results change every time you change the data. Each dynaset is temporary; it is not saved. Every time you query a database or change an existing query's design, Access creates a new dynaset.

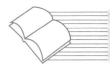

Now click on the Design View button to return to Design view, or choose Query Design from the View menu.

Selecting Specific Records

Now suppose you want only specific records from the table, such as those with today's tickle date. To do this, you must specify *criteria*.

 Criteria Criteria are conditions that a record must meet, or it's left out of the dynaset. As Access creates a dynaset, it will include only the records that meet the criteria you set. In our example, there is just one criterion: the tickle date.

You can use the Criteria row in the Query window to specify the conditions for record selection. If today's date is November 15, 1993, and you want records for only this date, you could enter 15-Nov-93 as the criterion in the column with the field name TICKLE. Notice that after you press Enter to complete the entry, the date format changes. Pound signs (#) are added as a prefix and suffix. (If you were doing a text match, as with the LNAME column, quotation marks would appear around the text.)

Now choose the Datasheet View button again. Only those records with the November 15 tickle date appear in the dynaset.

Specifying Additional Criteria

By adding and combining criteria in the Query window, you can do very powerful queries that meet complex conditions. If you have specified criteria for more than one field (for example, November 15, 1993 for TICKLE and 1 for REGION), a record must meet all the conditions for each field before the query will include it.

You can also specify to retrieve a record if either of two or more conditions is met (an *OR condition*). Assuming the salesperson was leaving town for a few days, you could specify as a condition of `>=15-Nov-93 OR<=17-Nov-93`. You could also specify a criterion as a list of values using the IN function, such as `IN(CA,WA)` for the ST field.

Saving the Query

When you have finished designing your query, save it by using the Save As command from the File menu.

Beware of Table Names   When you save your query, *do not use name of any table in your database*. Otherwise, the save will overwrite the table, and you will lose all your table data. You will get a warning message, but it's too easy to ignore the message if you're in a hurry.

In this lesson, you learned how to query a database. In the next lesson, you will learn how to modify and print the queried data.

Lesson 11

Modifying and Printing Queries

In this lesson, you will learn how to edit tables from a query, modify a query, calculate totals, and print the results of a query.

Editing Tables from a Query

When you use a query on a single table, you can edit the table directly from the displayed query. Display the query in Datasheet view, and edit it as you would the original table. To see your changes in the table, close the Query window and open the table.

Can't Edit a Query? If two or more tables are linked in a query, there may be ambiguity regarding which table contains the data. In that case, Microsoft Access may not let you edit the data in the query. (See Lesson 20.)

Modifying a Query

Queries can be modified to include new fields, new criteria, or reordered columns. Modify queries in Query Design view (see Figure 11.1).

Field list　　　　Field selector　　　　　　　　　QBE grid

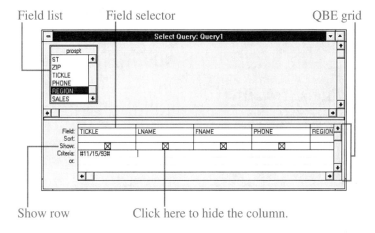

Show row　　　　　Click here to hide the column.

Figure 11.1　The Query Design window.

Selecting Columns

To add, delete, or insert columns, first you must select a column. This specifies where the action is to occur. To select a column, click on the *field selector* (which highlights the entire column).

Field Selector　The little box over the top cell of each column. When you click on this box, the entire column becomes highlighted.

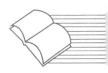

Modifying the Criteria

You can modify the criteria at any time by editing the Criteria row in the QBE grid.

 QBE Grid As you create a query, you use a table called a *QBE grid* to define grouping, sort order, and criteria.

Moving a Column

To move a column in a query, follow these steps:

1. Be sure you are in Query Design view.

2. Select the entire column you want to move.

3. Drag the column to the new location.

Deleting a Column

To delete a column in a query, follow these steps:

1. Be sure you are in Query Design view.

2. Select the entire column you want to delete.

3. Choose Delete from the Edit menu, or press the Delete key.

Inserting a Column

To insert a blank column into a query, follow these steps:

1. Select the column to the right of where you want to insert the new column.

2. Choose Insert Column from the Edit menu.

3. Choose a field name from the drop-down list box in the top cell.

Resizing a Column

To resize a column in a dynaset, drag the border of the field selector.

Hiding a Column

There may be times you want to hide a column in a query. For example, you may want to specify criteria for a field, but prefer not to display that field in the Datasheet view. To hide a column, go to that column in the QBE grid (in Design view), and click on the box in the row titled Show. The x will disappear from the box to show that the column will not be displayed in the dynaset.

Calculating Totals

You can also use a query to show totals. For example, assume the sales to each customer are added to the query, but you only want to see the total sales for each region. You would follow these steps:

1. Design your query grid so Access will use only the appropriate fields to do the calculations. For our example, you would delete all the columns except the REGION and SALES columns.

2. Click on the Totals button in the tool bar, or select Totals from the View menu. A new row called `Total` will appear just below the `Field` row (see Figure 11.2).

3. Click on the Total row, in the column you want to calculate. For our example, you'd click on the SALES column.

4. Use the drop-down list box to select the type of calculation you want. In our example, you want the total sales, so you'd select Sum.

5. To see the results of your query, click on the Datasheet View button, or select Datasheet from the View menu. In our example's dynaset, the SALES column will show the total sales for each region.

Click on this box for the drop-down list of calculation types.

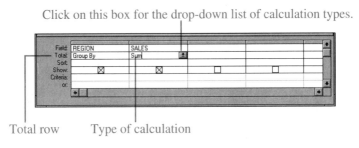

Total row   Type of calculation

Figure 11.2 Using a query to calculate totals.

Printing the Dynaset

If your query results are important, it's a good idea to have a printout of your dynaset, since Access won't save it. To print the dynaset, be sure the Query is in Datasheet view, then follow these steps:

1. Select Print from the File menu.

2. Select any option from the Print dialog box.

3. When you're finished selecting options, choose OK.

Print Preview If you want to see what your
dynaset will look like before it's printed, select
Print Preview from the File menu, or click on the
Print Preview button on the tool bar. You can view
different pages by clicking on the arrows at the
bottom left of the window. To exit, press Esc.

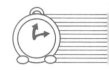

In this lesson, you learned how to modify a query,
calculate totals of columns, and print a dynaset. In the next
lesson, you will learn how to find data using a form.

Lesson 12

Finding Data by Using Forms

In this lesson, you will learn how to use forms to find specific data in tables, and how to use forms with filters to create subsets of data.

Tables, Forms, or Queries?

Using tables to find data has limitations. With a table, you can usually see only a few fields at a time. However, forms and queries allow you to get around the size limitations of a table. With a form you can find specific data, create subsets of data, sort data in a specific order, and locate data that meets specified criteria.

Using an Existing Form   The instructions in this lesson require that you use a form that has been created previously. If you haven't created a form yet, please refer to Lesson 8 to learn how.

Finding Data Using a Form

If you need to find data quickly, and you don't want to take the time to build a query, use a form. You can do a simple search, and locate the record you need. For example, suppose you need a telephone number for a certain prospect quickly. Let's see how to find it!

To find a value quickly, follow these steps:

1. Open the form from the Database window if it is not already open. (Select the form from the list, and either double-click on it or press Alt+O.)

2. Select the field to search by clicking on the title of the field, or by pressing the Tab key until the field is selected. For our example, you would select the PHONE field.

3. Click on the Find button on the tool bar, or choose Find from the Edit menu.

4. When the Find in field: dialog box appears, enter the data you wish to find in the Find What text box (see Figure 12.1).

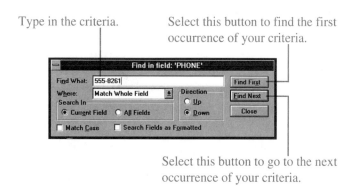

Type in the criteria.　　　　Select this button to find the first
occurrence of your criteria.

Select this button to go to the next
occurrence of your criteria.

Figure 12.1　Finding data with a form.

5. Choose any of the options listed in Table 12.1.

6. Choose Find First.

7. Access finds the first occurrence of the data you specified. If this is not the record you want, choose the Find Next button to move to the next occurrence.

8. When the search is complete, a dialog box will appear asking you if you want to start the search from the top again. Choose No, then close the Find in field: dialog box.

Can't See Your Form? If you can't see your form because the dialog box is in the way, move the dialog box by clicking on its title bar and dragging the box to a new location.

Table 12.1 Options for the Find in field: dialog box.

Option	Description
Where	Lets you choose from three options:
Any Part of Field	Matches the data you specified at every occurrence.
Match Whole Field	Matches exactly only the text you specify.
Start of Field	Finds only the matches that occur at the beginning of a field.
Current Field	Searches only the highlighted field.
All Fields	Searches every field.
Up	Searches toward the beginning of the table.
Down	Searches toward the end of the table.

Option	Description
Match Case	Finds only the matches that are in the same case as the data you specified.
Search Fields as Formatted	Finds matches based on how they appear on screen, not the format they were stored in.

Creating a Filter

You might want to display all the records that contain certain information instead of viewing them one by one with the Find command. Or you might want to specify criteria in more than one field. To accomplish either one, use a filter to create a subset of specific data.

Filter   A *filter* uses the data you specify to create a temporary datasheet of certain records (called a subset). A filter can be created only when you are using a form, never from a table or a query.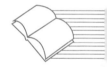

Subset   A *subset* is a group of records that contain the data you specified in the filter. The subset is similar to a query's dynaset.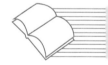

For example, suppose you had to create a subset of the prospects in Region 1 from the PROSPECT database. Follow these steps to create a filter:

1. Open the form from the Database window if it is not already open.

2. Click on the Edit Filter/Sort button on the tool bar, or choose Edit Filter/Sort from the Records menu.

3. The Filter window opens (see Figure 12.2). Notice that you can define criteria and select a sort order, but you can't perform calculations (as you can in a query).

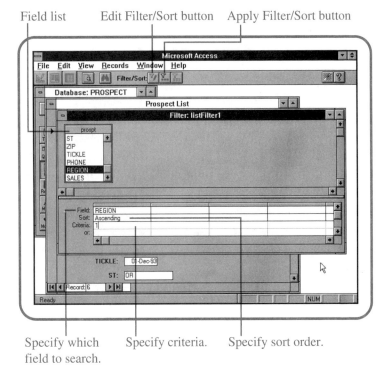

Figure 12.2   The Filter window.

4. From the field list, drag the desired field to the Field row. For our example, drag the REGION field to the first cell in the first column.

5. Enter the data you want Access to search for in the Criteria row. For our example, you would type the

number 1 in the Criteria row to tell Access to search for all of the REGION fields that contain the number 1 (see Figure 12.2).

6. Specify the sort order in the Sort row. In our example, you would choose Ascending so the prospects would be in alphabetical order.

7. To see the results in a subset, click on the Apply Filter/ Sort button on the tool bar, or choose Apply Filter/Sort from the Records menu (see Figure 12.3).

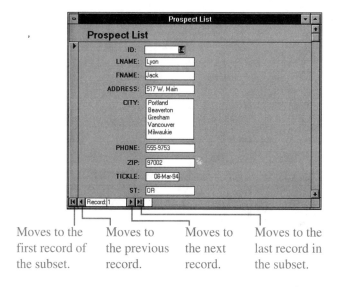

Moves to the first record of the subset. Moves to the previous record. Moves to the next record. Moves to the last record in the subset.

Figure 12.3 The result of using a filter.

Don't Panic!   Subsets, much like dynasets, are only temporary datasheets. When you create a filter, you are not changing your data in any way. Access is simply extracting the information you want from your table, and making it easier for you to view.

Saving a Filter

Because subsets are temporary, they cannot be saved. However, the filters that create the subsets can be saved as queries. To save a filter, select Save As Query from the File menu when you are in the Filter window. Name your filter, and then press Enter or click on OK.

Naming Filters When saving the filter as a query, don't use the name of any existing table, or the table and its data will be overwritten.

Using a Filter Saved as a Query

After you have saved a filter as a query, you can open it from a form whenever you want. You can also open it as a regular query from the Query list in the Database window. To open a filter from a form, follow these steps:

1. Click on the Edit Filter/Sort button on the tool bar, or select Edit Filter/Sort from the Records menu.

2. Select Load From Query from the File menu.

3. A dialog box will appear. Choose the filter you want to use, and click on OK or press Enter.

4. Click on the Apply Filter/Sort button on the tool bar, or select Apply Filter/Sort from the Records menu.

In this lesson, you learned how to find data by using the Find command and by using a filter. In the next lesson, you will learn how to create and use indexes.

Lesson 13
Using Indexes

In this lesson, you will learn how to create single-field and multiple-field indexes.

Creating Indexes

Indexes are used to access a specific record in a table quickly. If you have large tables, you will find that using an index speeds up the process of locating records. When you index a field, you are telling Access where to find the data, (as with an index in a book). Unlike subsets and dynasets, you cannot see an index. It is not a tool for viewing data, it is simply a way for Access to find your data more quickly.

Indexes are saved along with the table, and are changed automatically whenever you make changes in your fields. For this reason, it is probably not a good idea to use an index if you update your data often. When you change a lot of information, it can take Access quite a while to update the indexes. They are handy, however, if you search for data a lot—especially when you specify one or two particular fields in the search.

For example, say that you have a large table that stores records of clients. You search this table often for the last names of certain people, using the LNAME field. In this situation, using an index would allow you to find the data you need, quickly. To create an index, follow these steps:

1. Make sure you are in Table Design view.

2. Click on the field you want to index. Its properties will be shown in the window at the bottom of the screen. For our example, you would click on the LNAME field.

3. Click on the Indexed field in the Field Properties box.

4. Use the drop-down list box to select the conditions for your index. You can tell Access not to accept any duplicate values in the field, or you can specify that duplicates are okay (see Figure 13.1). In our example, you would choose Yes (Duplicates OK) because there might be more than one customer with the same last name.

Primary key field

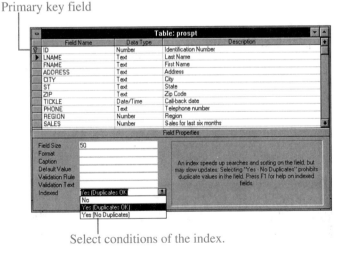

Select conditions of the index.

Figure 13.1 Creating an index for a field.

Primary Key Fields When you create a primary key field (see Lesson 4), Access automatically creates an index for that field. The index property will be set for Yes (No Duplicates) so that Access can use the primary key field to distinguish between the records in the table.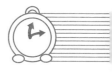

Multiple-Field Indexes

If you have a large table, you might search for records by using criteria in two different fields. In that case, you should consider creating indexes for the two (or more) fields you search most often.

For example, our sample table from the last section contains the names of our clients. If we have hundreds of records, chances are good that there are several people who have the same last name. If you are searching for a client named Susan Jones, it's easier for Access to filter through all the Joneses if you create an index for the FNAME field too.

To create a multiple-field index, follow these steps:

1. Make sure you are in Table Design view.

2. Click on the Properties button on the tool bar, or select Properties from the View menu.

3. The Properties box should show your primary key field and a list of fields labeled Index 1–5. Select Index1 if this is the only index you have.

4. In the Index1 field, type in the names of the fields to index separated by semicolons. For our example, you would type LNAME;FNAME (see Figure 13.2).

87

5. To create the index, save the table by selecting Save from the File menu.

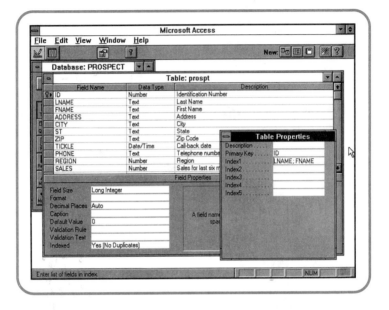

Figure 13.2 Creating a multiple-field index.

Deleting Indexes

You can create as many indexes as you need, but remember that using them will slow down the process of updating your records. You should index only those fields you search often. If you want to delete an index for a field that you don't search often, change the Indexed property to No by using the drop-down list in the Field Properties box.

To delete a multiple-field index, select the index you want to delete in the Table Properties box, and press the Delete key.

What Am I Deleting? When you delete an index, you aren't actually deleting anything. Your fields (and the data in them) remain exactly the same. You are simply telling Access that it doesn't have to remember where your records are for that field any more.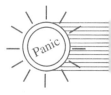

Searching for Records

Once you have created indexes, you can use the **Find** command to search for the data you need. To find a record from a table, follow these steps:

1. Click on the Find button on the tool bar, or select Find from the Edit menu.

2. The Find in field: dialog box will appear. Enter the data you wish to find in the Find What text box.

3. Choose any of the options listed for the Find in field: dialog box (for a list, see Table 12.1).

4. Choose Find First.

5. Access finds the first occurrence of the data you specified. If this is not the record you want, choose the Find Next button to move to the next occurrence.

6. When the search is complete, a dialog box will appear asking you if you want to start the search from the top again. Choose No, then close the Find in field: dialog box.

In this lesson, you learned how to use indexes. In the next lesson, you will learn how to create reports.

Creating and Using Reports

In this lesson, you will learn how to create a simple report from a table.

Using Reports

Reports are useful for communicating to people in an organized way. With Microsoft Access, one of the best ways to communicate your message is with a form or report. Lesson 8 showed you how to use forms to communicate your message. In this lesson, we'll look at using reports. Which should you use? Forms are useful for doing simple reports as well as viewing and editing your data. They are limited, however, in that you can't group data to show group and grand totals, you have less control over the layout, and you can't insert a report into a form. Reports can't be used to view or edit data, but you have more layout control, can group data for totals, and you can insert a report or graph into a report (see Lesson 17).

Creating a Report

Microsoft Access includes a ReportWizard feature which makes it simple to create reports from tables or queries. You will use it in this lesson to create a report from a table.

To create a report, open the database, if it is not already open, using Open Database on the File menu. When the Database window is displayed, choose the Report button at the left, then select New. A New Report window is displayed (see Figure 14.1).

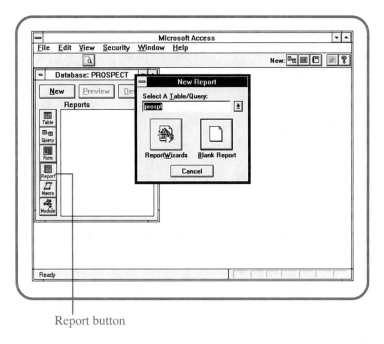

Report button

Figure 14.1 Starting to create a new report.

In the Select A Table/Query text box, click on the down arrow at the right or press Alt+↓. A list box will open, displaying available tables from which you can build reports. Click on the name of the desired table for the report. Now choose the ReportWizards button by clicking on it, or by pressing Alt+W. The following steps will help walk you through the ReportWizards:

1. On the first screen, select the AccessWizard you want to use. Choose Single-column, and then OK (see Figure 14.2).

2. Choose the fields for the report or select >> to move all the fields to the list box (see Figure 14.3). Then choose Next.

3. Choose the sort order from the fields (see Figure 14.4), and choose Next.

4. Choose the look for the report. For our example, choose Executive (see Figure 14.5) and click on Next.

5. Enter a title for the report (see Figure 14.6), and choose Print Preview.

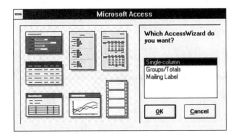

Figure 14.2   Choosing the layout for the report.

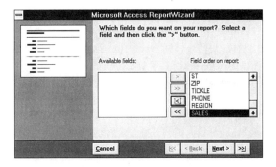

Figure 14.3   Choosing the fields to report.

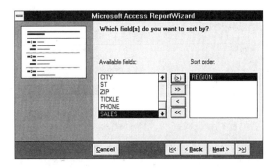

Figure 14.4   Choosing the sort order for the report.

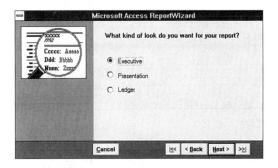

Figure 14.5   Choosing the style of the report.

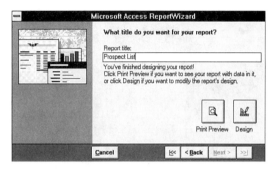

Figure 14.6 Entering the report title.

ReportWizard will then create the report and display a preview of what will print.

Previewing the Report

The preview mode gives you an idea of what the report will look like and the number of pages that will print before actually printing it. The pages will be magnified, and you can scroll through them using the horizontal and vertical scroll bars. You can use the Page buttons at the bottom of the window to scroll through the pages. The inside arrows move you a page at a time. The outside arrows move you quickly to the first or last page.

To see the entire page, move the cursor to the page (it becomes a small magnifying glass), and click. You can return to the magnified view again by clicking where you want to view.

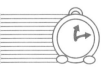

Preview You can always return to the Preview mode of a given report by choosing Print Preview from the File menu.

Printing the Report

You can print the report by choosing the Print button on the Print Preview window or by choosing Print from the File menu. A Print dialog box will be displayed. Set the options you wish, and then choose OK.

Saving the Report

After you have created the report, you should save it. To save the report, choose Save As from the File menu. Enter the name you wish to use for saving the report, and choose OK. Do not use the name of any existing table, query, or form.

In this lesson, you learned how to create a report. In the next lesson, you will learn how to create custom reports.

Creating
Custom Reports

In this lesson, you will learn how to customize a report form.

Modifying a Report Form

You can modify your report in various ways—moving items to other locations, resizing them, adding labels, and setting text attributes. To modify a report form, follow these steps:

1. Open the database, and choose the Report button in the Database window. Existing reports in the database are shown in the list.

2. Highlight the report you want to modify, and choose the Design button in the Database window. The report is displayed (see Figure 15.1) and can be modified, much like a form. The Toolbox is displayed by default, and you can turn on the Report Properties box by selecting Properties from the View menu.

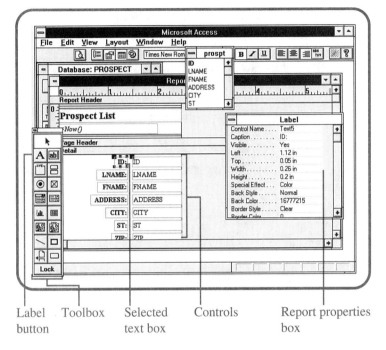

Label Toolbox Selected Controls Report properties
button text box box

Figure 15.1   The Report Design view.

Resizing Controls

Each object on the displayed report is a control. In the report's Design view, you can move and resize the controls, as well as add new controls.

Control   An object on a report or form that displays the data in a field, a calculation result, specific text, a graph, a picture, or another object.

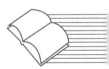

To manipulate a control, you must first select it. To select a text box with a label, click on the associated text box. The text box and its associated label will be displayed with handles (see Figure 15.1). The handles show as small black squares. Moving the mouse pointer to a handle will change the pointer to an arrow (when you are resizing the box) or a hand (when you are moving the box).

* To resize the box vertically, drag the top and bottom handles.

* To resize a box horizontally, drag the right and left handles.

* To resize a box horizontally and vertically at the same time, drag the diagonal handles.

Use the displayed rulers to align your work. You can select more than one control at a time by holding down the Shift key while clicking on them.

Moving Controls

Microsoft Access permits you to move a text box and its associated label together, or you can move each separately. To move a text box or label separately, select the control, and then drag the large handle in the upper left. This handle is known as the *move handle*. The cursor will be a pointing hand.

To move the text box and label together, click on a control until the pointer is a flat-palm hand, and drag the text box and its label to the new position.

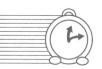 **Use the Rulers** The rulers can help with alignment when moving and resizing controls.

Adding a Label

A *label* is simply text that is added to the report at a later time to display information. The title already on the report is one type of label. You can add additional text, such as your company name, on the report. The label is not bound to any other control.

To add a label, you use the Toolbox that appears the first time you open a report in Design view. You can get the Toolbox, if it is not already displayed, by choosing Toolbox from the View menu. Click on the Label button at the left in the second row. Click in the report where you want the label, and enter the text for the label.

Customizing Text

You can modify any form text by changing the font, size, color, alignment, and attributes (normal, bold, italic). To change the appearance of text in a control, follow these steps:

1. Select the control to modify by clicking on it. If the control contains text, the tool bar displays additional tools for modifying the text (see Figure 15.2).

2. Click on any of the following buttons to customize.

Button	Function
Bold	Toggles boldface on or off.
Italic	Toggles italics on or off.
Underline	Toggles underlining on or off.
Left align	Sets the text to left alignment.

continues

99

continued

Button	Function
Center align	Centers the text in the margins.
Right align	Sets the text to right alignment.
Font	Selects the desired font.
Size	Sets the font size.

Figure 15.2   The tool bar for modifying text features.

3. To set the color of the text, click on the Palette button, or select Palette from the View menu. From the Palette window (see Figure 15.3), you can set the color of the text or you can set separate fill and outline colors. You can also set the appearance (normal, raised, sunken) of the text and the border width. To close the Palette window double-click on the small bar in the upper left of the window.

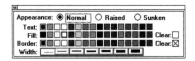

Figure 15.3   The Palette window.

4. After you have completed your work, choose Size to Fit from the Layout menu to resize the label to the new text.

100

Adding a Field to a Report

You can add fields to a report after it is created. Open the report in Design view and then open the field list. You can then drag fields to the appropriate place on the report.

Creating a Report with Grouped Data

You can use Microsoft Access to create reports with grouped data, showing subtotals and totals. For example, suppose you want to create a report showing sales by region with the grand sales total. You would use ReportWizard to create the report from the same table. Use this procedure:

1. Select Report from the Database window.

2. Choose New on the Database window.

3. On the New Report window, choose the PROSPT table from the list box, and then choose ReportWizard.

4. On the screen that selects the AccessWizard, select Groups/Totals. Choose OK.

5. On the new screen, select the fields to print and their order. Select ID, LNAME, FNAME, REGION, and SALES. Choose Next.

6. On the new screen, select to group by REGION. Choose Next.

7. On the new screen, select how to group as Normal. Choose Next.

8. On the next screen, set the sort order to SALES. Click on Next.

9. Set the Look to Executive (the default), and choose Next.

10. Enter the title, and choose Print Preview to see the report.

This procedure will create a report with the sales totaled by region, including a grand total.

In this lesson, you learned how to customize reports. In the next lesson, you will learn how to create mailing labels.

Lesson 16
Creating
Mailing Labels

In this lesson, you'll learn how to print simple mailing labels from your data in the database.

Introduction to Using Mailing Labels

The ability to create mailing labels is important for using address lists effectively. For example, you could print labels from the PROSPT prospect list created in Lesson 5, and use them to mail brochures or letters to the prospects.

Mailing labels come in many sizes and types. Some labels are designed for sprocket-feed printers that pull the labels through. Other labels come in sheets, and are designed for laser printers. Labels can also come in single, two, or three-column sizes. A two-up label, for example, means the labels are in two columns. Microsoft Access has the ability to print addresses with a wide variety of label types, and will support most of the common label sizes.

Use the Proper Labels for Your Printer! The adhesive gum used with standard peel-off labels does not work properly with the high temperatures of a laser printer. The labels can come off inside the printer and jam. Instead, use peel-off labels designed for laser printers.

Creating a Mailing Label Report

Using the Microsoft Access ReportWizard, you can create a special type of report that prints mailing labels. You can then save the report and use it again later.

This procedure will use examples from the table created in Lesson 5, or you can use any sample database with an address table (such as the Customer table in the NWIND database provided with Access). To create a report:

1. If the database is not already open, use Open Database on the File menu to open it.

2. When the Database window is displayed, choose the Report button at the left, then select New. A New Report window is displayed (see Figure 16.1).

Figure 16.1 The New Report window.

3. In the New Report window's Select Table/Query text box, click on the down arrow at the right, or press Alt+↓. A list box will open, displaying available tables and queries.

4. Click on the name of the desired table for the mailing labels. Now choose the ReportWizards button by clicking on it, or by pressing Alt+W. (Steps 5–9 walk you through the ReportWizard.)

5. On the first ReportWizard screen, choose Mailing Label and then click on OK (see Figure 16.2).

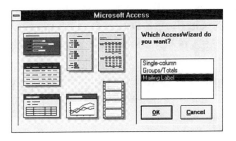

Figure 16.2 Choosing the mailing label report type.

6. From the Available fields list, choose the fields you want on the mailing label; using the right arrow, place them in the Label appearance box in the order you would like them printed.

7. Use the Punctuation buttons to enter the punctuation on the label. Here FNAME and LNAME are placed on the first line, ADDRESS on the next line, and CITY, ST, and ZIP on the third line. Punctuation is added as appropriate. Press the Return button between lines (see Figure 16.3). Choose Next.

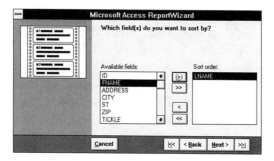

Figure 16.3 Entering punctuation on the mailing label.

8. Choose the sort order of the labels to print by placing the field names in the Sort order box, using the right arrow. Here the sort is by LNAME. Choose Next.

What If I Make a Mistake? If you make a mistake, use the backward arrow to clear the last change.

9. To choose the size of your mailing label, scroll to the correct size (see Figure 16.4), and select Next.

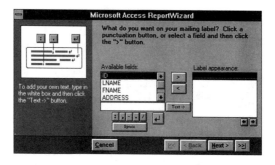

Figure 16.4 Choosing the mailing label size.

10. Select Print Preview from the last screen.

ReportWizard will then create the mailing label report, and display a preview of what will print.

Previewing the Report

The Preview mode gives you an idea of what the mailing labels will look like; the labels will be magnified. You can use the horizontal and vertical scroll bars to scroll through them, or the page buttons (at the bottom of the window). The inside arrows move you a "page" at a time; the outside arrows move you quickly to the first or last labels.

To see the entire "page," move the cursor to the page (it becomes a small magnifying glass) and click. You can return to the magnified view again by clicking where you want to view.

You can always return to the Preview mode of the mailing label report by choosing Print Preview from the File menu.

Printing the Mailing Labels

You can print the labels by following these steps:

1. Choose the Print button on the Print Preview window, or choose Print from the File menu. A Print dialog box will be displayed.

2. Set the options you want.

3. Choose OK.

Saving the Report

After you have created the label report, you should save it for future use. To save the report, follow these steps:

1. Choose Save As from the File menu.

2. Enter the name you want to use for saving the mailing label report. Do not use the name of any existing table, query, or form.

3. Choose OK.

In this lesson, you learned how to create and print mailing labels. In the next lesson, you will learn how to create graphs.

Lesson 17
Creating Graphs

In this lesson, you will learn how to add a graph to a report.

Introduction to Graphing

Graphs show information in visual relationships, and are especially useful for people who don't have time to read an entire report. A busy manager, for example, may find it quicker to look at a graph of sales by region than to decipher a statistical report.

Lesson 5's prospect database shows sales by region, so this lesson will refer to it. (You can use any database to try the procedure, including the Access samples; in that case, the database, table, and field names will be different.) First we will create a query on which the report will be based. Then we will create the report without the graph, using ReportWizard. Finally, we will use the Report Design view, and add the graph with a GraphWizard utility.

Creating the Query

First, let's create the query that shows sales by region. Open the database (if necessary); choose Query and New in the Database window.

1. In the Add Table window, choose PROSPT and click on the Add button.

2. Choose the Close button to close the Add Table window.

3. Scroll to find REGION in the list box. Drag REGION from the list to the first cell of the Field row of the grid.

4. Move SALES from the list to the next cell of the Field row of the grid.

5. Click on the Total button in the tool bar (or select Totals from the View menu) to add a Total row to the grid.

6. In the Total row, the cell under the Field row's SALES cell has the words Group By. Click on this Group By cell to open the drop-down list box, and choose Sum.

7. Click on the Datasheet View button to verify the totals in a dynaset.

8. Save the query (as SALESQ for this example), using the Save Query As command on the File menu.

9. Press F11 (or close the Query window) to return to the Database window.

Creating the Report

Now that this query has shown us sales by region, use ReportWizard to create a report based on the query.

1. Click on Report and then New in the Database window.

2. In the Table/Query text box, select the query you just created and saved (SALESQ).

3. Choose ReportWizards.

4. Select Single Column and OK.

5. On the next screen, choose the fields for the report. Select >> to move both the fields to the list box. Then choose Next.

6. On the next screen, choose the sort order (REGION) from the fields, and then select Next.

7. On the next screen, choose Executive and then Next.

8. On the next screen, enter a title and choose Print Preview. Verify that the report totals are correct.

Adding the Graph

Now add the graph to the report by following these steps:

1. Set the report to Design view by clicking on Cancel (if necessary) in the Print Preview window.

Get Back to Design You can always get to a report's Design view from a preview by clicking on Cancel.

2. Scroll down the Report window so that you have 2–3 inches of space under the footer section.

3. Click on the Graph button in the Toolbox (see Figure 17.1). If the Toolbox isn't showing, select it from the View menu.

Graph button —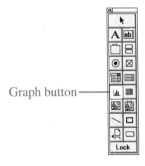

Figure 17.1 The Graph button in the Toolbox.

4. Using the mouse, drag to draw a control in the area below the report footer section for the graph. Make it about two inches high and six inches wide; use the rulers as necessary. (This will be the size not only of the control, but of the eventual graph.) When you complete the drag, a dialog box will be displayed (see Figure 17.2).

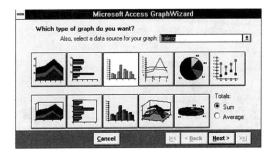

Figure 17.2 The Microsoft Access GraphWizard dialog box.

5. Now choose the data for the graph. In the text box, click on the arrow to open the list. Then choose the query on which you want to base the graph (SALESQ). Leave the default graph as two-column, and choose Next.

6. In the next box, select the fields for the graph. Choose SumOfSales and >, and then Next.

7. The next box asks whether to link the graph to the data; choose No. This means the graph won't change if the table's data is changed.

8. Enter the title on the next box, and choose the Design button.

Choose Print Preview on the File menu to see the report with the graph (see Figure 17.3).

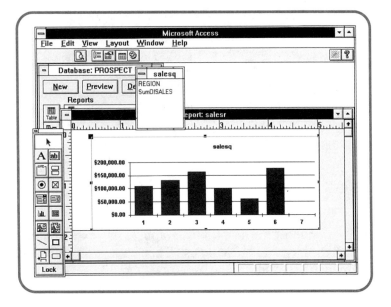

Figure 17.3 The final graph.

Editing the Graph

If you want to edit the graph, first Cancel any existing Print Preview window. Then double-click on the graph in Design view. This will open the graph in Microsoft Graph, a modular program that comes with Access (and resembles the chart mode of Excel, Microsoft's spreadsheet program). You can now add labels or titles, and even change the chart type, from the menu. To return to Access, choose Exit and Return to Microsoft Access from the File menu.

Printing the Report and Graph

You can print the report and graph by following these steps:

1. Choose the Print button on the Print Preview window, or choose Print from the File menu. A Print dialog box will be displayed.

2. Set the options you want.

3. Choose OK.

Saving the Report

After you have created the report and graph, you should save it. To save the report, follow these steps:

1. Choose Save As from the File menu.

2. Enter the name you want to use for saving the report. Do not use the name of any existing table, query, or form.

3. Choose OK.

In this lesson, you learned how to create a graph to use with a report. In the next lesson, you will learn how to use macros to automate your work.

Lesson 18

Automating Your Work

In this lesson, you will learn how to use macros to automate your work.

What's a Macro?

After you have used Microsoft Access for a short while, you will probably find you have a few tasks you do repeatedly—for example, opening a form and going to the end of a table to enter records. Such an action can be automated, so that a single command will set up the table for data entry. You can do this with a *macro*.

Macro   A list of actions you want Microsoft Access to perform for you automatically.

Creating a Macro

Let's say you want to create a macro that will open a frequently-used form (and table), and display an empty form at the end of the table for data entry. Open the database (use Open Database on the File menu), and then follow these steps:

1. Click on the Macro button in the Database window. Then choose New.

2. Click on the drop-down box in the Action column (see Figure 18.1) to see a list of available actions.

The Macro Window and Its Arguments   The *Macro window* is a two-column sheet for entering the actions you want the macro to execute. Many of these actions have *arguments*, additional information that you supply to specify how you want the action carried out.

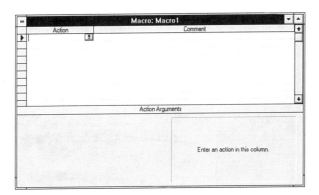

Figure 18.1   The Macro window.

3. From the Microsoft Access Window menu, choose Tile so you can see the Database window and the Macro window at the same time.

4. Choose Form on the Database window, and drag the desired form from the Database window to the upper left cell of the Macro window. When you release the mouse button, the word OpenForm will be in the cell. At the bottom of the Macro window, in an Action Arguments area, you can see the name of the form as the

117

Form Name, one of the arguments for this command (see Figure 18.2). When the macro executes this cell, Microsoft Access will open the associated form and its table.

5. Click on the second cell down and then the arrow to open the list box. Click on DoMenuItem to copy it to the Macro window. This puts the second command in the macro.

6. In the Action Arguments, click on the Menu Name Field (currently containing Edit) to see the drop-down menu items, choose Records as the Menu item. In the same way click on Command and choose Go To. Click on Subcommand and choose New. This puts the arguments in the second command (see Figure 18.3).

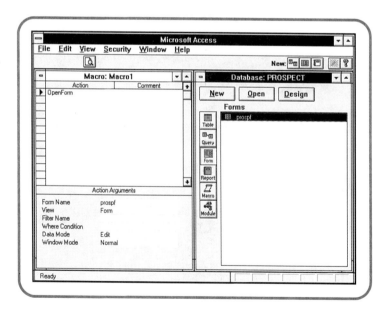

Figure 18.2 Entering the Action Arguments.

7. Save the Macro window, using Save As on the File menu. Enter a macro name, such as PROSPM. Click on OK.

8. Close the Macro window by choosing Close on the File menu with the Macro window active. The Database window should still be open.

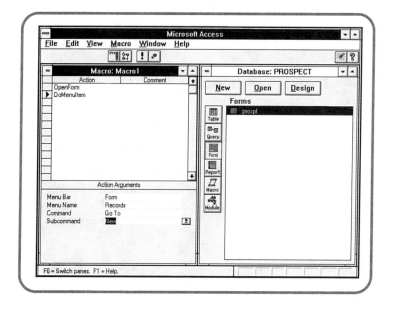

Figure 18.3   Editing the second command.

Executing the Macro

You have now created a macro and saved it (the macro must be saved before you can execute it). To execute the macro you have just created, follow these steps:

1. Choose Run Macro on the File menu.

2. Select the name of the macro.

3. Choose OK. Microsoft Access will open the table and form, and then display the form (positioned after the last record in the table), ready for a new entry.

There are other ways of executing a macro. For example, from the Database window you could select Macro, and double-click on the desired macro. Another method (when the Macro window is open) is to click on the exclamation point in the Macro window's tool bar.

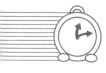 **Buttons for Launching Macros**   You can also use buttons to launch macro execution. For example, if you drag a macro name from the Database window to a form, you will see a new button on the form. You can click on this button to launch the macro. Using this trick, you can use a macro to open a second form, or copy data from a previous form entry to the current form entry (such as a city or state).

More with Macros

Once you have had some experience with Access, you can create macros for doing much of the routine work (for example, copying data from one form to another). They can do it faster, and help ensure it's done correctly.

In this lesson, you learned how to create and use macros in Microsoft Access. In the next lesson, you will learn how to share your data with other programs.

Lesson 19

Sharing Data with Other Programs

In this lesson, you will learn how to share data between Microsoft Access and other programs you may be using.

Importing, Exporting, and Attaching

You may already have data files for other programs such as Microsoft Excel, Lotus 1-2-3, dBASE IV, or Paradox. This data can be used with Microsoft Access to build reports, print mailing labels, and do queries. In Microsoft Access, you can manipulate data from other programs just as you can manipulate data created in Access. You can also use your Microsoft Access data with external programs (such as spreadsheets or other databases).

- When data in a Microsoft Access database table is transferred to an *external* database (or other program), this is called *exporting* the data. Access uses a table within the other program to create an external file that is compatible with it. Both files remain static; that is, updating one does not update the other.

External Database When you are importing data, an *external* database is one that is not a part of your open Microsoft Access database.

- When you transfer data from an external program to Microsoft Access, you are *importing* the data. Using the external program's file, Access creates an internal table it can use. Both files remain static; that is, updating one does not update the other.

- You can attach an external database to a Microsoft Access database. Although much slower than importing files, this process allows you to view, edit, or report from the other program's data as though it were in Microsoft Access, while staying within Access. There is a single file; users external to Access can use this file, even while you are updating or reporting from its data from within Access.

Exporting Data

When you export data, you are creating a file in the format of another program from a table in Microsoft Access. Beginning with an open database (such as PROSPECT), let's try an example: exporting a table in the format of dBASE (a Borland database product). Follow these steps:

1. Choose Export from the File menu.

2. In the Data Destination list box of the Export window, choose the destination format (see Figure 19.1). In this example, dBASE IV was chosen. Choose OK.

Figure 19.1   Choosing a format for the file to be exported.

3. In the Select Microsoft Access Object dialog box, choose the table name and select OK (see Figure 19.2). In this example, PROSPT was chosen.

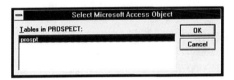

Figure 19.2   Choosing a name for the table to be exported.

4. In the Export to File dialog box, enter the name of the destination file (see Figure 19.3). Also select the drive and directory if necessary. Choose OK.

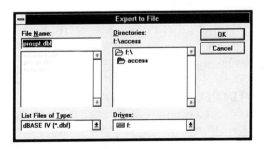

Figure 19.3   Choosing a name for the destination file.

123

The destination file will be created in the desired format. In this case the file PROSPT.DBF (a dBASE file format) will be created.

Importing Data

When you import data, you are creating a table in Access from a file that is another program. This external file could be in the format of Excel, Lotus 1-2-3, Paradox, dBASE IV, or even Microsoft Access (in another database). Let's see how to import the file we just created. Open a database (such as PROSPECT) if one is not already open.

1. Choose Import from the File menu.

2. In the Data Source list box of the Import dialog box, choose the type of input file to import (see Figure 19.4). Choose OK.

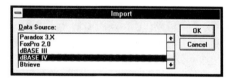

Figure 19.4 Choosing the type of file to import.

3. In the Select File dialog box, choose the drive and directory for the input file, and the name of the file you want to import (see Figure 19.5). Select Import.

4. After importing, the screen will display the message Successfully Imported *[filename]*. Choose OK in the message box. The message will vary with the type of file imported.

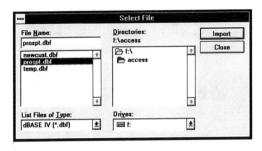

Figure 19.5   Choosing the file to import.

5. Close the Select File dialog box. The Database window will be displayed with the new table name.

Attaching Data

To use an external data file as if it were a table within Access, you can attach an external data file to Access. First open the desired database (such as PROSPECT) if it is not already open.

1. Choose Attach Table from the File menu.

2. In the Data Source list box of the Attach dialog box, choose the type of file you want to attach (see Figure 19.6). Select OK.

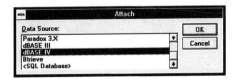

Figure 19.6   Choosing the type of table to be attached.

125

3. In the Select File dialog box, choose the drive, directory, and name of the file you are attaching (see Figure 19.7). Then select Attach.

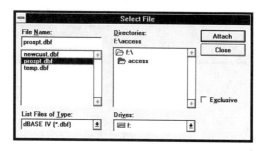

Figure 19.7 Choosing the file name for the table to be attached.

4. Select any necessary index file if requested, and choose Close when finished.

5. Access will tell you the file was attached successfully. Choose OK.

6. Choose Close on the Select File dialog box.

The table will be attached to your Access database, and you can use it for reports, queries, mailing labels, or graphs as you would any other table.

In this lesson you learned how to import tables to, export tables from, and attach tables to Microsoft Access. In the next lesson, you will learn how to minimize data duplication by joining tables.

Lesson 20
Joining Tables

In this lesson you will learn how to join tables to minimize data duplication.

Why Join Tables?

In the database example used in these lessons, a REGION code identified the sales areas for the prospects. It would be better to identify regions fully with text (such as Vancouver), but all that duplicated text would make the database's main table too large. It saves space to put the regions' full identification in a separate table, give each region a code, and use the region codes in the prospect table. Then we can join the two tables in a query, and have the query use the region codes to display the text that identifies each prospect. Now let's try it!

Create the Table

First, create the new table for the regions.

1. Open the database, and be sure the Tables button is selected. Then choose New. A Design view is displayed for a new table.

2. Enter `REGION` as a field, with a Number format.

3. Enter `REGION_NAME` as a field, with a Text format.

4. Select the REGION field, and in the Properties for this field, click on Format. Set the Format to Field Size.

5. Set the primary key by clicking in the REGION row, then clicking on the key in the tool bar (see Figure 20.1).

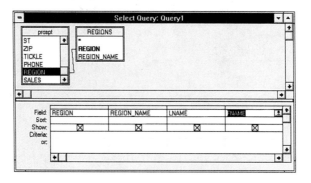

Figure 20.1 The REGIONS table.

6. Save the table as `REGIONS`, using Save As on the File menu.

7. Click on the Datasheet View button to view the datasheet; enter the data in the following way:

Under REGION:	Under REGION_NAME:
1	NE
2	Beaverton
3	Gresham
4	NW

Under REGION:	Under REGION_NAME:
5	SW
6	SE
7	Vancouver

8. Close the table to remove it from the screen.

9. In the Database window, select Query. Choose New.

10. In the Add Table dialog box, add the PROSPT and REGIONS tables to the query. The field list of both tables is displayed, with the primary keys in boldface. Choose Close.

11. Drag the desired fields to the Field row. Be sure both fields from the REGIONS table are included.

12. Click on the Datasheet View button. You will see the table is not correct for each region. This is because you haven't linked the tables yet.

13. Switch back to Design view by clicking on the Design View button. Click on the REGION field in the PROSPT list, and drag it to the REGION field in the REGIONS table list. When you release the mouse button, a line will connect the lists on the REGION field (see Figure 20.1).

14. Click on the Datasheet View button, and you will see the region names are now correct for each region.

If you save and close the query and table now, the link will remain. The next time you open the query, you will not need to reestablish the link.

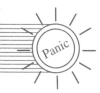

Link Trouble? Links can be a problem when you are editing a file from a query. If you need to do so and Microsoft Access won't let you, delete the link; reestablish it after editing.

Deleting a Link

To delete a link, click on the link to select it. Then press the Del key. The linking line will be deleted, and the tables will no longer be linked.

In this lesson, you learned how to create and delete links between tables. In the next lesson, you will learn how to manage your database.

Lesson 21
Managing Your Database

In this lesson you will learn how to copy, delete, back up, and repair your databases.

What Is Database Management?

Database management is a collection of procedures for maintaining your databases effectively and protecting their data. These activities include copying or deleting data as necessary, backing up the system, and repairing damaged databases.

Routine File Activities

There are routine chores associated with maintaining databases, such as copying, deleting, and renaming files. Microsoft Access stores all the objects of a database in a single file; its file name has an .MDB extension.

You can use the DOS COPY command to copy the database (as a single file) to another directory or drive, or to a floppy disk. To copy the PROSPECT database from

C:\ACCESS to A:\PROSPECT, for example, you would enter this command line at the DOS prompt:

```
COPY C:\ACCESS\PROSPECT.MDB A:\PROSPECT
```

For more information on the COPY command, see your DOS manual.

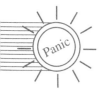

Whoops! I Accidentally Deleted a Database! You can rename a database from the DOS prompt with no problems, but *use caution when deleting*. If you delete a database accidentally, your only hope for recovery is using the UNDELETE command in DOS—and it may not work. See your DOS manual for more instructions on using this command.

To delete a database, use the DEL command from the DOS prompt. To delete a SALES.MDB database, for example, enter:

```
DEL SALES.MDB
```

Another Way to Delete Files You can also copy and delete files from the Windows File Manager.

Deleting Objects To delete an object (table, report, etc.) from a database, choose the object, and then choose Delete from the Edit menu.

In the same way, you can rename a database from the DOS prompt with the REN command. For example:

```
REN PROSPECT.MDB SALES.MDB.
```

132

Backing Up Your Data

When using Microsoft Access, it's wise to back up your databases frequently. You should always back up a database before making important changes (such as modifying a table structure, or making design changes to queries, reports, or forms). A backup might involve nothing more than copying the current database to a file in the same directory, using a different name. This can be done quickly from the Windows File Manager. (See the Appendix for information on Windows File Manager.)

Back Up Regularly   The entire system should be backed up periodically, using software designed for this purpose. To prevent data loss from fire, flood, or other catastrophe, keep the media used for the backup somewhere else—at a separate geographic location. Do this on a regular schedule and stick to it, no matter how busy you get. The most likely time to lose data is when you are very busy, because it's harder to be careful then.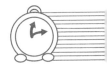

Save It Safely!   Be careful not to duplicate names when you save tables, queries, and other objects in a database. *Saving a query under the same name as a table will cause the loss of the table data.*

Repairing a Database

As you use Microsoft Access, keep your databases closed unless you are using them. Display only the startup screen until you need the database open for use. Any time the database is open, it can be damaged if there is a power loss or power surge. There is the same risk if the computer locks up, forcing the user to reboot.

Microsoft Access will detect previous damage the next time you open the database. If the database is damaged, a message will appear and alert you to the need for repair. Choose the OK button to have Access attempt repair. Once this is done, check the last changes you made, and be sure these were completed. You may have to reenter some data, or redesign a form or report.

A database can also be damaged in a way Microsoft Access cannot detect. In this case, choose Repair Database from the File menu to force a repair of the database.

If all else fails, copy your backup database files to the hard disk again. If the Microsoft Access program becomes corrupted, it can be installed again from the floppy disks.

Congratulations! You've learned how to use Access to create databases, enter and edit data, build forms, use queries, and create reports. For more information, see the Microsoft Access *Getting Started* and *User's Guide*.

Microsoft
Windows
Primer

Microsoft Windows is a *graphical interface* program that makes your computer easier to use. It enables you to select menu items and pictures instead of typing commands. Learning some basics will help you take advantage of Windows' capabilities.

Starting Microsoft Windows

To start Windows, do the following:

1. At the DOS prompt, type `win`

2. Press Enter.

The Windows title screen appears for a few moments, and then you see a screen like the one in Figure A.1.

What If It Didn't Work? You may have to change to the Windows directory before starting Windows; to do so, type `CD \WINDOWS` at the DOS prompt, and press Enter.

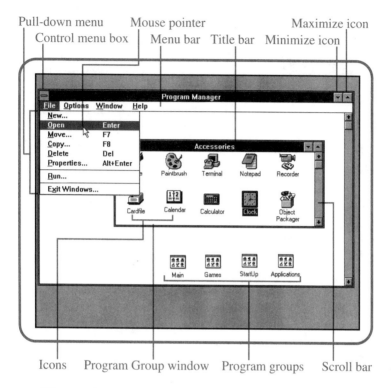

Figure A.1   The Windows Program Manager.

Parts of a Windows Screen

As shown in Figure A.1, the Windows screen contains several elements that you won't see in DOS. Here's a brief summary.

- *Title bar*   This shows the name of the window or program.

- *Program Group windows*   These contain program icons, which allow you to run programs.

- *Icons* These are graphic representations of programs. To run a program, you select its icon.

- *Minimize and Maximize buttons* These alter a window's size. The Minimize button shrinks the window to the size of an icon. The Maximize button expands the window to fill the screen. When maximized, a window contains a double-arrow *Restore button*, which returns the window to its original size.

- *Control menu box* When selected, this pulls down a menu that offers size and location controls for the window.

- *Pull-down menu bar* This contains a list of the pull-down menus available in the program.

- *Mouse pointer* If you are using a mouse, this pointer (usually an arrow) appears on-screen. It can be controlled by moving the mouse (as discussed later in this appendix).

- *Scroll bars* These appear if a window contains more information than can be displayed in the window. *Scroll arrows* on each end of a scroll bar allow you to scroll slowly. The *scroll box* allows you to scroll more quickly.

Using a Mouse

To work most efficiently in Windows, you should use a mouse. You can press mouse buttons and move the mouse in various ways to change the way it acts:

Point means to move the mouse pointer onto the specified item by moving the mouse. The tip of the mouse pointer must be touching the item.

Click on an item means to move the pointer onto the specified item and press the mouse button once. Unless specified otherwise, use the left mouse button.

Double-click on an item means to move the pointer onto the specified item, and then press and release the mouse button twice, quickly.

Drag means to move the mouse pointer onto the specified item, hold down the mouse button, and move the mouse while holding down the button.

Figure A.2 shows how to use the mouse to perform common Windows activities, such as running applications and moving or resizing windows.

Starting a Program

To start a program, simply select its icon. If its icon is contained in a Program Group window that's not open at the moment, open that window first. Follow these steps:

1. If necessary, open the Program Group window that contains the program you want to run. (To open the window, click on its icon.)

2. Double-click on the icon for the program you want to run.

Using Menus

The *pull-down menu bar* (see Figure A.3) contains various menus from which you can select commands. Each Windows program that you run has a set of pull-down menus; Windows itself has a set too.

Click here to control window size and location.   Drag title bar to move window.   Click here to shrink.   Click here to expand.

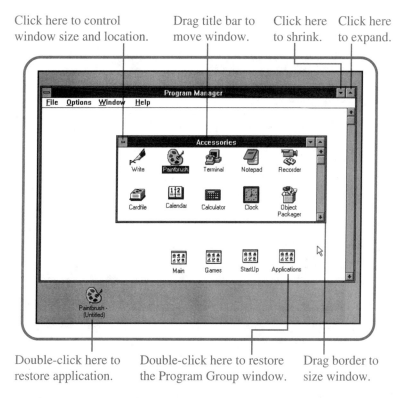

Double-click here to restore application.   Double-click here to restore the Program Group window.   Drag border to size window.

Figure A.2   Use your mouse to control Windows.

To open a menu, click on its name on the menu bar. Once a menu is open, you can select a command from it by clicking on the desired command.

Accelerator Keys   Notice that in Figure A.3, some commands are followed by key names such as Enter (for the **O**pen command) or F8 (for the **C**opy command). These are called *accelerator keys*. You can use these keys to perform these commands without even opening the menu.

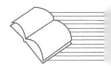

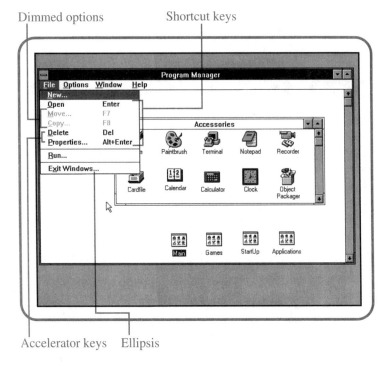

Figure A.3   A menu lists various commands you can perform.

Usually, when you select a command, the command is performed immediately. However:

* If the command name is *gray* (rather than black), the command is unavailable at the moment, and you cannot choose it.

* If the command name is followed by an *arrow*, selecting the command will cause another menu to appear, from which you select another command.

* If the command name is followed by an *ellipsis* (three dots), selecting it will cause a dialog box to appear.

140

(You'll learn more about dialog boxes in the next section.)

Navigating Dialog Boxes

A *dialog box* is Windows' way of requesting additional information. For example, if you choose Print from the File menu in Write, you'll see the dialog box shown in Figure A.4.

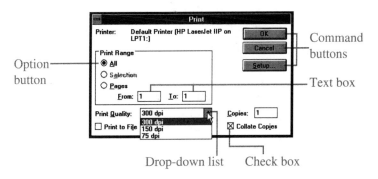

Figure A.4 A typical dialog box.

Each dialog box contains one or more of the following elements:

- *List boxes* display available choices. To activate a list, click inside the list box. If the entire list is not visible, use the scroll bar to view the items in the list. To select an item from the list, click on it.

- *Drop-down lists* are similar to list boxes, but only one item in the list is shown. To see the rest of the items, click on the down arrow to the right of the list box. To select an item from the list, click on it.

- *Text boxes* allow you to type an entry. To activate a text box, click inside it. To edit an existing entry, use the arrow keys to move the cursor, and the Del or Back-space keys to delete existing characters, then type your correction.

- *Check boxes* allow you to select one or more items in a group of options. For example, if you are styling text, you may select Bold and Italic to have the text appear in both bold and italic type. Click on a check box to activate it.

- *Option buttons* are like check boxes, but you can select only one option button in a group. Selecting one button deselects any option that is already selected. Click on an option button to activate it.

- *Command buttons* execute (or cancel) the command once you have made your selections in the dialog box. To press a command button, click on it.

Switching Between Open Windows

Often you will have more than one window open at once. Some of these may be Program Group windows, while others may be actual programs that are running. To switch among them, you can:

- Pull down the Window menu and choose the window you want to view.

- If a portion of the desired window is visible, click on it.

Controlling a Window

As you saw earlier in this appendix, you can minimize, maximize, and restore windows on your screen. But you can also move them and change their size.

- To move a window, drag its title bar to a different location. (Remember, "drag" means to hold down the left mouse button while you move the mouse.)

- To resize a window, position the mouse pointer on the border of the window until you see a double-headed arrow, then drag the window border to the desired size.

Copying Your Program Diskettes with File Manager

Before you install any new software, you should make a copy of the original diskettes as a safety precaution. Windows' File Manager makes this process easy.

First, start File Manager by double-clicking on the File Manager icon in the Main program group. Then, for each disk you need to copy, follow these steps:

1. Locate a blank disk of the same type as the original disk, and label it to match the original. Make sure the disk you select does not contain any data you want to keep.

2. Place the original disk in your diskette drive (A or B).

3. Open the Disk menu and select Copy Disk. The Copy Disk dialog box appears.

4. From the Source In list box, select the drive used in step 2.

143

5. Select the same drive from the Destination In list box. (Don't worry; File Manager will tell you to switch disks at the appropriate time.)

6. Select OK. The Confirm Copy Disk dialog box appears.

7. Select Yes to continue.

8. When instructed to insert the Source diskette, choose OK, since you already did this at step 2. The Copying Disk box appears, and the copy process begins.

9. When instructed to insert the target disk, remove the original disk from the drive, and insert the blank disk. Then choose OK to continue. The Copying Disk box disappears when the process is complete.

Index